FROM HORSES TO HORSEPOWER

FROM HORSES TO HORSEPOWER

THE MECHANIZATION AND DEMISE OF THE U.S. CAVALRY 1916-1950

ALEXANDER BIELAKOWSKI

FONTHILL

For Rae: now it is your turn!

Fonthill Media Language Policy

Fonthill Media publishes in the international English language market. One language edition is published worldwide. As there are minor differences in spelling and presentation, especially with regard to American English and British English, a policy is necessary to define which form of English to use. The Fonthill Policy is to use the form of English native to the author. Alexander Bielakowski was educated in the United States; therefore American English has been adopted in this publication.

Fonthill Media Limited
Fonthill Media LLC
www.fonthillmedia.com
office@fonthillmedia.com

First published in the United Kingdom and the United States of America 2019

British Library Cataloguing in Publication Data:
A catalogue record for this book is available from the British Library

ISBN 978-1-78155-721-1

Typeset in 10.5pt on 13pt Sabon
Printed and bound in England

Acknowledgments

While researching this manuscript, I almost worked in more archives than I can actually remember, but I must especially acknowledge the assistance of the following individuals: Mitch Yokelson and Tim Nenninger at the National Archives and Records Administration, College Park, Maryland; Dr. Richard Sommers and David Keough at the U.S. Army Military History Institute, Carlisle Barracks, Pennsylvania; Alan Aimone at the United States Military Academy Archives, West Point, New York; and Terry Van Meter, William McKale, and Robert Smith at the U.S. Cavalry Museum and Archives, Fort Riley, Kansas.

Glossary and Abbreviations

Armored:	Generally, this term referred to any vehicles that had armor plating designed to protect the crew. Most commonly, however, it referred to tanks.
Armored Car:	A wheeled vehicle built on a truck or car chassis to which armor plating was added to protect the crew.
Combat Car:	The U.S. Cavalry used this term to refer to tanks, because the Cavalry branch was prohibited from owning tanks under the National Defense Act of 1920. In reality, combat cars and tanks were almost identical in design.
Mechanized:	This term generally referred to any vehicles that had caterpillar tracks, rather than wheels. Nevertheless, the term was also used more loosely to refer to any vehicles which were both armored and motorized.
Motorized:	A term used generally to refer to any vehicles that were powered by an internal combustion engine. In military parlance, however, it usually referred to vehicles that were driven on wheels, rather than with caterpillar tracks.
Tank:	An armored and mechanized vehicle, which usually mounted a gun (20 mm and up) and/or several machine guns (.30 and .50 calibers).

Photo Abbreviations

ISCARL:	Ike Skelton Combined Arms Research Library, Fort Leavenworth, Kansas.
LC:	Library of Congress, Washington, DC.
NARA:	National Archives and Records Administration, Washington, DC.
USCM:	U.S. Cavalry Museum, Fort Riley, Kansas.

Contents

Acknowledgments 5
Glossary and Abbreviations 6
Introduction 9

1 U.S. Cavalry in the Mexican Punitive Expedition and World War I 19

2 Mechanization in the Interwar U.S. Cavalry 36

3 "Traditionalists": Proponents of the Horse 65

4 "Modernizers": Proponents of Mechanization 99

5 "Pragmatists": Attitudes Among the Army's Future Leaders 119

6 "Compromiser": Patton's Approach to Mechanization 137

7 U.S. Cavalry in World War II and the Post-War U.S. Army 159

Conclusion 174
Endnotes 185
Bibliography 200
Biography 208

Introduction

Following World War I, horse cavalry entered a period during which it fought for its very existence against mechanized vehicles. On the Eastern Front during the war, horse cavalry saw combat, which influenced the interwar military theory of Eastern European nations. On the Western Front, however, the stalemate of trench warfare became the defining image of the war throughout the world. While horse cavalry remained idle in France, the invention of the tank and its potential for success led many non-cavalry officers to accept the notion that the era of horse cavalry had passed. Nevertheless, military technology required almost another generation to equal the intellectual expectations of its supporters.

During the interwar period, a struggle raged within the U.S. Cavalry regarding its future role, equipment, and organization. Some cavalry officers argued that mechanized vehicles supplanted horses as the primary means of combat mobility within the cavalry, while others believed that the horse continued to occupy that role. The response of prominent cavalry officers to this struggle influenced the form and function of the U.S. Cavalry during World War II. This study examines the struggle within the cavalry branch during the interwar period to determine how cavalry officers dealt with the evolving intellectual and cultural crisis. These sorts of changes are a perennial challenge to military professionals and almost always involve a struggle between competing ideas and cultures. In recent years, the U.S. Army has debated technological change in the form of Network Centric Warfare and the proposed Future Combat System. Likewise, military intellectuals continue to debate ideas such as Design, Mission Command, and Full Spectrum Operations. Change in a large bureaucratic organization like the Army is difficult because these organizations tend to resist change. By examining the attitudes and actions of cavalry officers in the interwar period, however, military professionals of the twenty-first century facing an uncertain future may be able to avoid the most painful aspects of change and allow for a more streamlined process of technological and organizational innovation.

The interwar evolution of technology necessitated important changes in military culture that some officers found difficult to accept. Before World War I, the career of

Colonel Selah "Tommy" Tompkins was a legendary officer who served with the 7th Cavalry Regiment for thirty-one of his thirty-four years on active duty. Directly commissioned as a second lieutenant by President Chester Arthur at the age of nineteen, Tompkins fought American Indians on the frontier, Spaniards in Cuba, Moros in the Philippines, and the soldiers of Francisco "Pancho" Villa in Mexico. (*USCM*)

a U.S. Army cavalry officer was markedly similar to that of his nineteenth-century father and grandfather. Almost all of these officers were West Point graduates, and the exceptions tended to be graduates of Norwich University, the Virginia Military Institute, the Citadel, or the Agricultural and Mechanical College of Texas (now Texas A&M University)—all military academies that inculcated officers with "traditional" military culture. The training that they received at these institutions changed very little from the nineteenth century and emphasized the Army's historical continuity.

Service conditions reinforced the historical continuity these officers encountered during their initial military training. Before World War I, officers served in a close-knit, almost family-like environment in which they literally knew (at least by name and reputation) every other officer in their branch (cavalry, field artillery, infantry, etc.). Most were the sons and/or grandsons of Army officers, and often they were related by blood or marriage to other officers. In addition, since the military conflicts of the post-frontier period (the 1890s to 1916) so closely resembled the Indian fighting of the post-Civil War period, the career experiences of these officers closely resembled that of their fathers and grandfathers.[1]

Above: Members of Troop F, 6th Cavalry Regiment, at Yosemite Valley National Park in California. (*LOC*)

Right: Major General Samuel B. M. Young volunteered for service during the Civil War and finished the war as a brevet brigadier general at the age of twenty-six. He joined the regular army after the war and he retired in 1904 as the first U.S. Army Chief of Staff. (*USCM*)

Moreover, the equipment and training of these officers changed only marginally from the post-Civil War period to the Regular Army that entered World War I in 1917. A reliable bolt-action rifle (M1903) finally replaced the single-shot (M1873/M1884) Springfield trapdoor of the post-Civil War period, while a semi-automatic pistol (M1911) replaced the "saber charge" with the "pistol charge." Nevertheless, the machine gun was still a seldom issued and more seldom used item, while literal "horse power" was the only method of transporting men or supplies from the railroads to the battlefield. In the realm of training, many officers had little or no formal military training beyond the undergraduate level. While early incarnations of the Command and General Staff College, including the School of the Line and the Army Staff College, did exist at that point, their influence on the officer corps was only beginning to be felt throughout the Army. At that time, less than 25 percent of Army officers had any graduate-level military education and the majority of those who did were in the infantry.[2]

The last campaign of the Army before the entry of the United States into World War I was also an example of historical continuity in the lives of these cavalry officers. The Mexican Punitive Expedition closely resembled the many campaigns against the Apaches in the American Southwest during the post-Civil War period. The life of a cavalry officer in the period immediately preceding World War I, therefore, changed little from that of a similar officer in the post-Civil War period.[3]

The use of motorized vehicles during World War I served as a significant break in these officers' sense of historical continuity, providing a glimpse of the mechanically dominated battlefields of the future. Mass armies and technologically-driven mass killing were the dominant images of World War I. The almost complete absence of horse cavalry on the battlefield and its seeming replacement by tanks served as a jarring discontinuity for American cavalrymen who had, only a year earlier, participated in such a traditional campaign in Mexico. Nevertheless, during the interwar period, many cavalry officers attempted to return to the comforts of pre-World War I traditionalism, despite their wartime experiences. As a result, cavalry officers grappled with the intellectual and cultural struggle between the combat utility of both the horse and the mechanical vehicle.

Among cavalry officers, there were distinct responses to the issue of mechanized development during the interwar period. The first response supported horse warfare, despite its possible obsolescence. The second response supported mechanized warfare, although its future effectiveness remained in question. Confronted with these two responses, a third response was to maintain professional links with competing pro-horse and pro-mechanization factions until the fate of horse warfare was finally decided by a combination of international and internal events in 1940. The fourth response was uniquely embraced by one cavalry officer, who supported both horses and mechanized vehicles with varying degrees of vigorousness throughout the interwar period. Ultimately, the rationale of the first response was "traditionalist"; the second, "modernizing"; the third, "pragmatic"; and the fourth, "compromising."

This work investigates the progress of this struggle through an examination of seven of the most prominent cavalry officers of the period: Adna R. Chaffee, Jr.,

Cavalrymen of Troop B, 6th Cavalry Regiment, Fort Riley, Kansas, in 1896. (*USCM*)

Troopers from the 4th Cavalry Regiment during the Philippine Insurrection, *c.* 1902. (*USCM*)

Above: Cavalrymen of Troop M, 6th Cavalry Regiment, at the Great Wall of China during the Boxer Rebellion in 1900. (*USCM*)

Left: Dapper looking officer of the 7th Cavalry Regiment, *c.* 1910. (*USCM*)

Hamilton S. Hawkins, Guy V. Henry, Jr., John K. Herr, Leon B. Kromer, George S. Patton, Jr., and Daniel Van Voorhis. These officers were selected because they had the greatest impact, either positive or negative, on the process of mechanization. Chaffee was both the best connected (his father had been the U.S. Army Chief of Staff) and the least likely (he was an Olympic-level horseman) advocate for mechanization. Hawkins was the oldest and most senior supporter of the horse. Henry and Kromer were the Chiefs of Cavalry who were advocates for mechanization. Herr was the only Chief of Cavalry to oppose any and all efforts to replace horses with motorized and mechanized vehicles. Patton—the most famous officer in this group—held perhaps the most complex views regarding the issue of mechanization. Lastly, Van Voorhis was the oldest (he first joined the Army during the Spanish–American War) and most senior advocate for mechanization.

This study attempts to determine how cavalry officers dealt with the evolving intellectual and cultural crisis during the interwar period. In order to accomplish this task, one must recognize the human and often flawed perspectives among these cavalry officers. This work acknowledges the very real tensions among these officers, examines the evolution of their thought throughout the interwar period, and evaluates their influence on the mechanization process.

While other authors have examined cavalry mechanization during the interwar period, they have taken different approaches in their discussions. The two

Second Lieutenant Adna R. Chaffee, Jr., *c.* 1908. (*LOC*)

Above: Cavalry officer members of the U.S. Olympic Team on June 3, 1924. (*LOC*)

Below: Two cavalry troopers practicing fencing, *c.* 1916. (*USCM*)

most important published works are Robert S. Cameron's *Mobility, Shock and Firepower: The Emergence of the U.S. Army's Armor Branch, 1917–1945* (U.S. Army Center of Military History, 2008) and George F. Hofmann's *Through Mobility We Conquer: The Mechanization of U.S. Cavalry* (University of Kentucky Press, 2006). The focus of Cameron's book is to detail the emergence of the Armor branch. In this work, the Cavalry branch is treated briefly and only as an antecedent of the Armor branch. Hofmann's book remains the single most comprehensive work on the subject of the interwar U.S. Cavalry. However, Hofmann's approach does not delve as deeply into the ways that the human dimension shaped the process of mechanization. The current work seeks specifically to examine the roles of individuals in the process of change to determine how cavalry officers dealt with the evolving intellectual and cultural crisis caused by mechanization.

1

U.S. Cavalry in the Mexican Punitive Expedition and World War I

During the twentieth century, technological innovations (including the internal combustion engine and heavier-than-air flight) significantly altered warfare. The U.S. Cavalry dealt with this change starting with the Mexican Punitive Expedition of 1916. For instance, during the Punitive Expedition, horse cavalrymen for the first time coordinated their operations with trucks and airplanes. Then soon after the end of the Expedition, many cavalrymen found themselves serving in Europe in a war that saw the horse reduced to the status of nothing more than a draft animal. American cavalrymen reacted to these changes with a seemingly odd combination of indifference and adaptability.

The Mexican Punitive Expedition was the American response to the raid by Mexican revolutionary Francisco "Pancho" Villa on Columbus, New Mexico, on March 9, 1916, in which seventeen American soldiers from the 13th Cavalry Regiment were killed. Following the raid, President Woodrow Wilson ordered Brigadier General John J. Pershing into Mexico to find and capture Villa and his men. The Punitive Expedition was principally a horse cavalry campaign. The cavalry troopers endured the same sorts of hardships as their predecessors who battled Cochise, Geronimo, Victorio, and other North American Indians of the Southwest: rough, irregular terrain; an arid climate; and the necessity of spending entire days on end in the saddle.[1] The Punitive Expedition was significant both for being the last horse-mounted campaign in American history and the first U.S. Army campaign to use mechanical vehicles.

The Army units designated to participate in the Punitive Expedition formed a provisional division with two provisional cavalry brigades and one provisional infantry brigade. The 1st Provisional Cavalry Brigade consisted of the 11th Cavalry Regiment, 13th Cavalry Regiment, and Battery C, 6th Field Artillery Regiment. The 2nd Provisional Cavalry Brigade consisted of the 7th Cavalry Regiment, 10th Cavalry Regiment, and Battery B, 6th Field Artillery Regiment. The 1st Provisional Infantry Brigade consisted of the 6th Infantry Regiment, 16th Infantry Regiment, and Companies E and H, 2nd Engineer Battalion.[2] The officers

Left: Trooper from the 16th Cavalry Regiment stationed along the Mexican border, *c.* 1916. (*USCM*)

Below: Cavalrymen from Troop G, 1st Cavalry Regiment, at Naco, Arizona, 1915. (*USCM*)

Machine guns of the 8th Cavalry Regiment in action during the Mexican Punitive Expedition in 1916. (*LOC*)

who served on Pershing's staff and among the regiments included a veritable "who's who" of men who later became senior Army leaders during World Wars I and II—such as John L. Hines (U.S. Army Chief of Staff, 1924–26), Leon B. Kromer (Chief of Cavalry, 1935–37), and George S. Patton, Jr.

The Punitive Expedition dragged on for almost a year of hard campaigning, with numerous chases and small skirmishes, but only one real "battle" with Villa's troops. On March 29, 1916, at Guerrero in the state of Chihuahua, the 7th Cavalry Regiment finally caught up with some of the Villistas. Villa had himself been in Guerrero the day before the Americans arrived, but in a brief firefight with Mexican federal troops, he was shot in the right leg by one of his own men and evacuated.[3] Colonel George A. Dodd, commander of the 2nd Provisional Cavalry Brigade, planned to surround Guerrero on three sides and then drive the Villistas toward the "open" side of town, where they would be met by troopers from the 7th Cavalry Regiment. As it happened, however, the Americans lost the element of surprise and instead fought a running battle over very difficult terrain against the Villistas, who tried desperately to retreat. Of the 370 Americans engaged, only five were lightly wounded, while thirty-five of the 500–600 Villistas were killed with an unknown number wounded.[4]

Unsurprisingly, since Villa was never captured, nearly everyone, both in the Army and in the civilian leadership in Washington, D.C., deemed the Punitive Expedition a failure. The real significance of the Punitive Expedition for the Army, however, was the first ever combination of trucks and airplanes on a campaign with horse cavalry. Unfortunately, most Army officers believed that the trucks and airplanes failed to prove their worth during the Punitive Expedition. In fact, after

Left: Troop C, 5th Cavalry Regiment, at Lozier Canyon, Texas, *c.* 1916. (*USCM*)

Below: The 11th Cavalry Regiment on the march through Mexico during the Punitive Expedition on April 27, 1916. (*LOC*)

Right: Corporal Richard Tannous of the 13th Cavalry Regiment who was shot through the arm at Parral, Mexico, during the Mexican Punitive Expedition in 1916. (*LOC*)

Below: Brigadier General John J. Pershing (fourth from the left) and his staff during the Mexican Punitive Expedition in 1916. Second from the left is 1st Lieutenant James L. Collins, who would be a major general in World War II and whose brother, Joseph L. Collins, was the Chief of Staff of the U.S. Army from 1949 to 1953. (*USCM*)

only a single month, all eight of the 1st Aero Squadron's aircraft were damaged beyond repair and the unit returned home almost six months before the end of the campaign.[5] In the aviators' defense, Lieutenant Colonel Charles S. Farnsworth, an infantry officer who commanded the Base of Communications for the Punitive Expedition, complained that "the Aero Squadron was badly handicapped by poor equipment."[6] Despite his defense of the 1st Aero Squadron, Farnsworth believed that horse cavalry rather than aircraft should have been assigned to him:

> The Base of Communications not being provided with any Cavalry, the Aero Squadron was utilized for frequent reconnaissance ... for distances about equal to a day's march of Cavalry. A Base of Communications should be provided with sufficient Cavalry for local reconnaissance.[7]

The commander of the 1st Aero Squadron, Captain Benjamin D. Foulois, defended his unit's record by pointing out that they were the first aviation unit to participate in active field service.[8] In addition, the 1st Aero Squadron was issued aircraft designed for civilian operation (and produced by five different manufacturers) and was understrength in equipment, particularly trucks, from the beginning of the Punitive Expedition.[9]

Criticisms were also directed toward the trucks that accompanied the Punitive Expedition. In all, the Army organized ten truck companies for the Punitive Expedition, but there was no standardization among the thirteen truck models from seven different automobile manufacturers and repair parts were often not available.[10] Many officers viewed the frequent breakdown of these trucks and the need to transport fuel, oil, and spare parts to keep the trucks operating as a waste of resources. Even the Punitive Expedition's senior engineer officer, Lieutenant Colonel Meriwether L. Walker, complained that "difficulty was encountered in keeping truck trains moving."[11] Captain Francis H. Pope, a cavalryman who served as the Punitive Expedition's S-4 (Logistics), prepared a formal report on the truck companies and enumerated the limitations under which the truck companies operated. He pointed out that, as with the 1st Aero Squadron, the Punitive Expedition represented the first active field service of truck companies with the Quartermaster Corps. Pope, therefore, saw the Punitive Expedition as training that provided invaluable experience for the Quartermaster Corps during subsequent operations in World War I.[12] While many officers in the cavalry and infantry considered the trucks a failure, the Quartermaster Corps itself thought completely the opposite.[13]

Despite the opinions of aviators and quartermaster officers, the worth of both airplanes and trucks in the Punitive Expedition remained debatable to many in the Army. Trucks also failed to live up to expectations during experiments conducted in the United States.[14] As far as most Army officers were concerned, horses and horse cavalry remained viable as long as Mexico continued to be a possible theater of operations and until such time as American industry delivered reliable vehicles. Indeed, the War Department stressed this notion in its preparations to

Above: Trooper, 2nd Cavalry Regiment, *c.* 1916. (*USCM*)

Right: Then-Lieutenant Colonel Charles Young while commander of the 2nd Squadron, 10th Cavalry Regiment during the Mexican Punitive Expedition in 1916. Young was the third African American graduate of West Point and the first African American to reach the rank of full colonel. (*ISCARL*)

Aerial view of the Motor Truck Group, at Fort Sam Houston, Texas, in December 1916. (*LOC*)

Troopers and pack horses from the 12th Cavalry Regiment. (*USCM*)

send the American Expeditionary Force to Europe. Since infantry and artillery were more suitable for the conditions on the Western Front, they were sent in large numbers, while cavalry was retained in the United States to patrol the border with Mexico.[15]

The Punitive Expedition ended in February 1917 and the United States entered World War I just two months later in April. By the time the United States declared war on the Central Powers, the war was almost three years old and the conflict had taken on a rather distinct character. On the Western Front, cavalry faced limitations imposed by terrain and technological innovation and, though both sides maintained cavalry in reserve, these horsemen remained basically idle after the opening phase of the war in 1914. In contrast, the Eastern Front offered more opportunities for cavalry action, which had a significant effect on interwar military development in some Eastern European nations.[16] The United States, however, found itself operating almost exclusively on the Western Front and conformed to the dominant style of warfare in that theater. In World War I, trucks, airplanes, and the newest addition to the military arsenal, the tank, evolved and became pivotal in the execution of the war, while cavalry found itself on the sidelines without a significant role to play.

In May 1917, the regular U.S. Cavalry was organized into seventeen regiments (numbered 1st through 17th), while emergency legislation called for the organization of an additional eight Regular Army regiments (numbered 18th through 25th) and fifteen National Army regiments (numbered 301st through 315th). Almost immediately, the War Department realized that cavalry regiments were in far less demand in France than artillery regiments. Thus, the eight new Regular Army cavalry regiments were converted to field artillery regiments (redesignated 76th through 83rd), while the National Army cavalry regiments were converted to field artillery and trench mortar units.[17] In addition, National Guard cavalry regiments spent World War I either on the Mexican border or converted into field artillery regiments for duty on the Western Front.

Despite the circumstances, four cavalry regiments (2nd, 3rd, 6th, and 15th Cavalry) did see service in France. These regiments, however, tended to be used for remount and military police duties. In November 1917, Pershing, by then a full general and the commander the American Expeditionary Force (AEF) in France, requested the organization of a cavalry division for use after the expected breakthrough was made in the German lines (i.e., in the traditional cavalry pursuit role). In December 1917, in response to this request, Secretary of War Newton D. Baker authorized the creation of the 15th Cavalry Division with nine cavalry regiments organized into three cavalry brigades. As the reality of war on the Western Front became obvious to the War Department, however, the division's organization was never completed and the division itself was disbanded in May 1918.[18]

The one exception to rule about American cavalry on the Western Front was the 2nd Cavalry Regiment, which participated in the Aisne-Marne, Saint-Mihiel, and Meuse-Argonne offensives.[19] In late August 1918, a Provisional Squadron,

Motorcycle Detachment, 1st Cavalry Regiment, El Paso, Texas, *c.* 1916. (*USCM*)

Practice charge of the 8th Cavalry Regiment at Fort Bliss, Texas, in 1916. (*LOC*)

Troopers of the 13th Cavalry Regiment leaning on Brigadier General John J. Pershing's staff car during the Mexican Punitive Expedition, 1916. (*USCM*)

Cavalry drill at Fort Ethan Allen, Vermont, in May 1918. The 18th and 19th Cavalry Regiments were formed at Fort Ethan Allen, before being reflagged at the 76th and 77th Field Artillery Regiments. (*NARA*)

Left: Horseshoer James Toland, Troop L, 8th Cavalry Regiment, Camp Marfa, Texas, *c.* 1916. (*USCM*)

Below: Sergeant Samuel MacDonald with troopers of the Troop G, 2nd Cavalry Regiment, Fort Riley, Kansas, *c.* 1929. (*USCM*)

composed of Troops B, D, F, and H of the 2nd Cavalry, was organized with Lieutenant Colonel Oliver P. M. Hazard as the commander.[20] Hazard, a veteran of the Philippine Insurrection, was unable to command the squadron in the field because he suffered from debilitating bouts of amoebic dysentery. As a result, Captain Ernest N. Harmon, the commander of Troop F, was the *de facto* squadron commander when it went into action.[21, 22]

The Provisional Squadron, 2nd Cavalry Regiment, amounted to only fourteen officers and 404 enlisted men. After spending ten days retraining for mounted action at Camp Jeanne d'Arc, near Neufchâteau, the squadron was ordered to the front. Soon afterward, Troop B was detached for courier duty between the 1st, 42nd, and 89th Divisions, while the remainder of the squadron was attached to the 1st Division.[23] Beginning on September 4, 1918, the remainder of the squadron performed reconnaissance duty for the 1st Division. However, due to the condition of the battlefield and enemy resistance (they encountered retreating German soldiers who, using machine guns, routed them), the squadron was generally unsuccessful at reconnaissance. Thereafter, and through the Saint-Mihiel (September 12–16) and Meuse-Argonne (September 26–November 11) offensives, the squadron mostly acted as couriers and military police with only brief reconnaissance duties. On October 17, the squadron, reduced to only 150 mounted troops (mostly as a result of sick or wounded horses), was withdrawn from the line.[24]

Since the 2nd Cavalry was the only American cavalry regiment to see combat during World War I, most cavalry officers looked elsewhere to find active service. The vast majority of cavalry officers who saw combat in the war served as infantry and field artillery officers. Since the field artillery was still horse-drawn, cavalry officers easily transferred their skills from horse cavalry to horse artillery. Nevertheless, the infantry was the most popular branch of service for cavalry officers wishing to see combat in World War I, because it was the primary combat arm of the war and offered the most opportunities. In addition, since American cavalry trained extensively for dismounted combat, cavalry officers easily transitioned to the infantry. For some cavalry officers, however, neither the artillery nor the infantry seemed appropriate. For these individuals, the newly created Tank Corps seemed a better fit. The most famous of these cavalry officers was George S. Patton, Jr., who rose to the temporary rank of colonel and was awarded the Distinguished Service Cross for valor while commanding a tank brigade.[25] After the war, like most other cavalry veterans of the Western Front, he returned to the cavalry, which they believed remained a viable and important arm of the Army.

For the cavalry, the results of World War I were mixed at best. For some officers, even those who, like Patton, served with the Tank Corps, the war did not mean the end for the horse. Officers from many different nations and branches of service continued to regard horse cavalry as a viable military arm. Pershing stated in 1922 that "There is not in the world today an officer of distinction, recognized as an authority in military matters in a broad way who does not declare that cavalry is

Troop F, 2nd Cavalry Regiment, *c*. 1916. (*USCM*)

Machine Gun Troop, 13th Cavalry Regiment, Camp Stewart, Texas, March 20, 1917. (*ISCARL*)

Chaplain blessing the colors of the 310th Cavalry Regiment at Fort Ethan Allen, Vermont, on June 25, 1918. Four months later, the regiment was later broken up and its troopers used to organize the 58th and 59th Field Artillery Regiments and the 20th Trench Mortar Battery. (*LOC*)

an important as arm today as it has ever been."[26] General Charles P. Summerall, the U.S. Army Chief of Staff, stated in 1927 that "There has been a great deal of misinformation broadcasted relative to the Cavalry. It is a fact that cavalry is of far more importance than it has ever been before."[27] These opinions regarding the cavalry were not reserved to the U.S. Army. French Marshal Philippe Pétain, the hero of the Battle of Verdun, stated in 1920 that "The cavalry remains the favored arm for reconnaissance and screening before the battle, and for the exploitation of success after the battle."[28] British Field Marshal George Allenby stated in 1921: "I have never felt more confidence in the future of our arm than I do today. It has retained the good, rejected the bad, and has not shrunk from the new."[29] Even German Field Marshal Paul von Hindenburg stated after the war that "Cavalry will continue to be important."[30] For some senior officers, therefore, horse cavalry remained a respected and important arm of the military arsenal even after World War I.

Despite the opinions of eminent military officers, World War I altered warfare forever. Whether in the form of aircraft or tanks, technological change was the most prominent feature of the war. For a variety of reasons, the majority of cavalry officers entered the interwar period committed to the horse and somewhat disdainful of technological innovation despite the results of World War I.[31] However, other officers, both cavalry and non-cavalry, began to advocate experimentation with new technologies.

PRO
PATRIA!
WELSH
1917
JOIN
ARMY FOR
PERIOD OF
WAR.
THE HEGEMAN PRINT N.Y.

Brigadier General John J. Pershing inspecting the camp of the 5th Cavalry Regiment in New Mexico during the Mexican Punitive Expedition in 1916. (*LOC*)

Opposite: Cavalry recruiting poster from World War I. (*LOC*)

2

Mechanization in the Interwar U.S. Cavalry

On June 2, 1920, less than two years after the end of World War I, the U.S. Congress passed the National Defense Act of 1920, which defined the organization of the armed forces during the interwar period. Rather than creating a new and more powerful peacetime U.S. Army, the Act returned the Army to the *status quo ante*, chronically under-funded and only large enough to serve as a skeleton for future wartime buildups. The Act, which had a major effect on both interwar tank development and cavalry modernization, officially establishing three new branches of the Army (Air Corps, Chemical Warfare Corps, and Finance Corps), while at the same time abolishing one wartime branch (Tank Corps). All of the Army's tanks were assigned to the infantry, while the cavalry was prohibited from possessing tanks.[1] Unfortunately, the Act did not reflect a change in national military policy, but rather a continuation of the *de facto* standing policy since the American Revolution. Historically, Americans were hostile to any large standing army regardless of changed geopolitical circumstances or the consequences on the state of military preparedness or national defense.

The National Defense Act's reorganization of the cavalry branch resulted in both positive and negative changes for the branch and process of modernization. The cavalry was reorganized into seventeen Regular Army cavalry regiments (1st to 17th Cavalry Regiments), twenty-one National Guard cavalry regiments (101st to 117th and 121st to 124th Cavalry Regiments), and twenty-four Organized Reserve cavalry regiments (301st to 324th Cavalry Regiments). These regiments were further organized as two Regular Army divisions (1st and 2nd Cavalry Divisions), with the later addition of another Regular Army division (3rd Cavalry Division) and a separate brigade (7th Cavalry Brigade), four National Guard divisions (21st to 24th Cavalry Divisions) and a separate brigade (56th Cavalry Brigade), and six Organized Reserve divisions (61st to 66th Cavalry Divisions). However, almost all of these organizations (above the regimental level) in the Regular Army and National Guard units, as well as most of the Organized Reserve cavalry regiments, brigades, and divisions, existed almost exclusively on paper.[2]

U.S. Army Tank Corps recruiting poster in World War I. (*LOC*)

Troop F, 1st Cavalry Regiment, New York National Guard, practicing cavalry charge at Manor Farm, on Staten Island in May 1916. The regiment was later broken up to form the 102nd Trench Mortar Battery and the 104th and 106th Machine-Gun Battalions. These units saw combat with the 27th Division in World War I. (*NARA*)

The National Defense Act of 1920 created a bleak two-decade-long period for the Army as a whole. Rather than an expansion beyond the pre-World War I force levels, there was actually a contraction of forces. As the 1920s wore on, War Department budgetary reductions in the cavalry included: a decrease in the strength of cavalry regiments from twelve to only six lettered troops organized into two squadrons; the inactivation of the 15th, 16th, and 17th Cavalry Regiments; the consolidation of the 117th Cavalry Regiment (Colorado National Guard) into the 102nd Cavalry Regiment (New Jersey National Guard); the re-designation of the 2nd Squadron, 122nd Cavalry Regiment (Connecticut and Rhode Island National Guard), as the 2nd Battalion, 103rd Field Artillery Regiment (Rhode Island National Guard); and the consolidation of the remainder of the 122nd Cavalry into the 110th Cavalry Regiment (Connecticut, Massachusetts, and Rhode Island National Guard).[3] The only additions and improvements in the cavalry during that era, other than the "paper" brigades and divisions, were the creation of the Office of the Chief of Cavalry (organized at the same time as the branch chiefs of each of the other combat arms) and the formation of the 26th

Cavalry Regiment (Philippine Scouts). The 26th Cavalry, organized in 1922 from personnel of the 25th Field Artillery Regiment (Philippine Scouts) and stationed at Camp Stotsenburg, Philippine Islands, included American officers and Filipino enlisted-men.[4]

Since money for research and development was almost non-existent and the most sophisticated tanks were gas-guzzling, slow-moving, and subject to frequent breakdowns, the senior leadership in the War Department believed that tanks were nothing more than mobile machine-gun emplacements.[5] As a result, mechanization in the U.S. Army languished during the 1920s. Only a few individuals maintained the spark of interest in mechanization within the Army.

J. Walter Christie remains a controversial and enigmatic figure in the history of mechanized development, but the innovative nature of his designs is unquestioned. Beginning in 1880, he trained as a machinist at the De Lamater plant in New York City, which produced the engines for the USS *Monitor* during the Civil War. Christie then began working on race cars as early as 1901.[6] During World War I, he created his first military vehicles—trucks and motorized gun carriages. In early 1918, since American soldiers were equipped with British and French tanks, Christie began to experiment with the idea of designing the first American tank. In November 1919, Christie's "steel steed" (as he called it) made its debut at the Aberdeen Proving Grounds in Maryland. The Model 1919 Christie tank was years ahead of almost every other tank in the world, but with World War I over, the Army's Ordnance Department had no funds for external projects and rejected the design.[7]

Undaunted by the Army's rejection of his design, Christie created the world's first amphibious tank in 1921. When the Army proved disinterested in the amphibious tank, he approached Brigadier General Smedley D. Butler of the U.S. Marine Corps. With permission from the Marine Commandant, Major General John A. Lejeune, Butler used the amphibious tank in an exercise at Culebra Island, Puerto Rico. Despite the amphibious tank's success in the exercise, the Marine Corps also decided not to purchase the tank.[8] Christie was now almost broke, having spent $296,000 of his own money to design vehicles rejected by both the Army and Marine Corps. As a result of his financial situation, Christie was forced to sell the plans for his amphibious tank to the Japanese government, who offered him $25,000.[9] Christie resisted the sale because he wanted his designs used by the United States, but his creditors gave him no choice.

Between 1926 and 1929, Christie designed and manufactured a hybrid truck/tractor very similar to the M2/M3/M5 halftracks of World War II. This vehicle, which he called the "Christie Crawler," proved to have commercial as well as military applications and Christie found himself in the black financially for the first time since prior to World War I. Though the Army tested the "Crawler" at Aberdeen and found it more than met their needs, it was returned to Christie with the comment that the Ordnance department did not have sufficient funds to purchase it.

On July 4, 1928, Christie debuted a completely new tank design, the Model 1928 Christie tank, before hundreds of spectators, reporters, and even newsreel

Soldiers from the 101st and 103rd Field Artillery Regiments pose in front of a monastery which was serving as a YMCA, in Rangeval, France, on April 29, 1918. One battalion of the 103rd Field Artillery was originally organized as 1st Separate Squadron, Rhode Island Cavalry, and would later again be designated as a cavalry squadron. (*NARA*)

U.S. Army FT17 tank crewed by Sergeant Edward White and Corporal Edward J. Elliot, in France, September 27, 1918. (*LOC*)

Inventor J. Walter Christie's M1919 tank. (*LOC*)

Inventor J. Walter Christie's amphibious tank undergoing experiments with the U.S. Marine Corps, 1924. (*LOC*)

On May 5, 1924, inventor J. Walter Christie unveiled a newly designed motorized gun carriage. (*LOC*)

Christie M1928 tank. (*USCM*)

cameras. The Model 1928 engaged in a series of stunt maneuvers so amazing that Christie's son later claimed that then-Major George S. Patton, Jr., shouted, "If the Army doesn't buy it, I will!"[10] The Model 1928 had a system of individually sprung wheels with a coil-spring, knee-action suspension, which allowed for stunts that would have reduced every other contemporary tank to a pile of scrap metal.

Patton and Major Clarence C. Benson, the cavalry members of a board of officers appointed to evaluate the Model 1928 Christie tank, supported the adoption of the design. Christie's tank appeared to be everything that the cavalry had long thought impossible: a mechanized vehicle capable of fast cross-country movement to support horse cavalry formations.[11] Unfortunately, the Ordnance Department, which had ultimate authority in the selection of new equipment, refused to formally adopt the Model 1928 Christie tank—though a few vehicles were purchased for evaluation.

Despite the genius displayed in Christie's designs, the man himself was not without some significant faults. Convinced that his designs were perfect, he resisted even the most minor of changes—even when they determined whether or not he was able to sell the vehicle. The design for Christie's suspension system was eventually adopted and adapted by the Soviet Union, where it became the basis for the BT-series of tanks in the 1930s and later the T34 tank of World War II, and the United Kingdom, where it became the basis for Crusader tank.[12] In both cases, Christie was again forced to sell his designs to satisfy his creditors. J. Walter Christie died on January 11, 1944, bankrupt and living off the charity of his family and friends.

Another individual who had a significant role in interwar mechanization was Dwight F. Davis, the Secretary of War from 1925 to 1929. While on a tour of the

Christie tank undergoing testing on June 11, 1936. (*LOC*)

Another view of a Christie tank. (*LOC*)

United Kingdom in 1927, Davis was fascinated by the British Army's Experimental Mechanized Force, which he observed on maneuvers on the Salisbury Plain. This force consisted of an armored car battalion, a tank battalion, a motorized machine-gun battalion, artillery (both truck-towed and self-propelled), motorized engineers, and limited support from the Royal Air Force.[13] Upon his return to America, Davis ordered the formation of the U.S. Army's own Experimental Mechanized Force at Camp Meade, Maryland, for the purpose of exploring the possibilities of mechanization.

The War Department laid out the basic principles to be followed during the maneuvers of the Experimental Mechanized Force. The Force was a completely self-contained unit, which combined mobility and striking power in a form unmatched by the existing arms. The Force was not a traditional division-sized combat element but rather an exclusively offensive special missions unit. During the Force's intended one-year life span, it was supposed to be a tactical and technical laboratory to experiment with mechanization.[14] Davis, therefore, gave the Force a free hand to experiment with any and all ideas related to mechanization.

Almost all branches of the Army sent units or representatives to Camp Meade to participate in the mechanized experiment. The Experimental Mechanized Force consisted of 1st Battalion, 34th Infantry Regiment, which was mounted on trucks produced during World War I; 2nd Battalion, 6th Field Artillery Regiment (less one battery), which was equipped with 75-mm Howitzers and also mounted on World War I-vintage trucks; an engineer company; a signals company; an anti-aircraft battery; a chemical warfare company; an ammunition train; an Air Corps observation squadron; a medical detachment; 16th Tank Battalion (Light), equipped with World War I French-designed M1917 tanks; 17th Tank Battalion (Heavy), equipped with World War I British-designed Mk VIII or "Liberty" tanks; and the cavalry contribution, the only armored car troop in the entire U.S. Army.[15]

From July to September 1928, the Experimental Mechanized Force participated in maneuvers at Camp Meade. As time wore on, however, the old equipment broke down, until near the end of September, with no money in sight to procure new equipment, the War Department discontinued the mechanized "experiment." The decision was made because "little could be done tactically until [the Army] had more modern equipment."[16] Many in the news media, which heavily covered the Force, and in the Army considered the "experiment" a complete failure. Others, however, believed that the Force operated under severe limitations and wanted the "experiment" to be given another chance under better circumstances. In fact, the *Washington Post* editorialized on just that point:

> It has been proved that a motorized force is superior to one that is not. But a force mounted on broken-down equipment cannot prevail against an army mounted in modern, up-to-the-minute machines. It has been demonstrated that the need is imperative for increased appropriations for mechanization. Congress should not refuse any request for such funds.[17]

British Mark IV tank named "Britannia," which was brought to New York City and put on exhibit to help sell war bonds. This photo shows the tank taking part in the Liberty Loan Parade on October 25, 1917. (*LOC*)

U.S. Army Mark VIII tanks, Camp Meade, Maryland, 1922. (*LOC*)

U.S. Army FT17 tanks in France 1918. (*LOC*)

Soldiers and horse drawn caissons waiting at the side of a narrow road while tanks pass in France, 1918. (*LOC*)

In 1930, the War Department Mechanized Development Board, after spending over a year studying the data accumulated during the maneuvers of the Experimental Mechanized Force in 1928, recommended that the Mechanized Force be reestablished and made a permanent part of the Army. The Board stated:

> In the commercial world the machine has largely replaced man-power; so, in the Army must we, to the fullest practical degree, use machines in place of man-power in order that our man-power can occupy and "hold" without terrific losses incident to modern fire-power.[18]

The Board recommended that the new Force include: two battalions of motorized infantry, one battalion of motorized field artillery, one light tank battalion, one armored car cavalry troop, one motorized chemical corps company, one motorized engineer company, and one motorized anti-aircraft detachment.[19] The Board's recommendations, however, were just that—recommendations—not binding upon the Army.

In October 1930, a month before his retirement, U.S. Army Chief of Staff General Charles P. Summerall, acting on the War Department Mechanized Development Board's recommendations, ordered the establishment of a permanent Mechanized Force at Fort Eustis, Virginia. A cavalry officer, Colonel Daniel Van Voorhis, commanded the "permanent" Force, with the result that though the Force was technically independent, most cavalry officers now believed that they "controlled" the Force's development. After all, the cavalry was well armed and highly mobile, just like the Mechanized Force. In just a matter of months, the cavalry's aspirations for control of the new Force came true when in May 1931, the new Chief of Staff, General Douglas MacArthur, decided that the Army still lacked the funds necessary to develop an independent mechanized arm and therefore disbanded the Mechanized Force and transferred much of its assets to the cavalry.

MacArthur believed that because the cavalry was the traditional arm of mobility and maneuver, it was the natural place for mechanized forces. He also thought that it was a misconception to believe that the cavalry needed to include horses. MacArthur's reasoning:

> Modern firearms have eliminated the horse as a weapon, and as a means of transportation he has generally become, next to the dismounted man, the slowest means of transportation. In some special cases of difficult terrain, the horse, properly supplemented by motor transportation, may still furnish the best mobility, and this situation is properly borne in mind in all our plans.[20]

MacArthur foresaw the complete reorganization and re-equipping of the cavalry into two types of regiments. Traditional cavalry regiments, relying on horses and mules, would exist only in those cases in which the horse and mule could not be replaced due to anticipated operations in difficult terrain or on unique tactical

U.S. Army Mark VIII tank on maneuvers in 1922. (*LOC*)

In May 1927, U.S. Army Chief of Staff General Charles P. Summerall poses with corps and division commanders at the War Department in Washington, D.C.
Left to right, front row: Major General Douglas MacArthur, III Corps; Major General William Lassiter, VI Corps; Major General James H. McRae, II Corps; Summerall; Major General John L. Hines, IX Corps; Major General Ernest Hinds, VIII Corps; and Major General Hanson E. Ely, Commandant of the War College.
Left to right, back row: Major General Harry A Smith, Assistant Chief of Staff; Major General Dennis E. Nolan, V Corps; Brigadier General Edwin B Winans, 1st Cavalry Division; Major General Malin Craig, IV Corps; Major General Fox L. Connor, I Corps; final two men unknown. (*LOC*)

On February 5, 1935, U.S. Army Chief of Staff General Douglas MacArthur testifies before the House Military Affairs Committee on the "Take the Profits Out of War" Resolution. (*LOC*)

missions. The second type of cavalry regiment formed with tanks, armored cars, and trucks would represent the majority of cavalry regiments.[21]

As a result of MacArthur's decision, the Army disbanded the Mechanized Force for a second time and used its assets to mechanize a cavalry regiment. However, this decision met with hostility from many cavalry officers. Even Van Voorhis protested that the decision doomed mechanization to become a mere curiosity within the cavalry. On the other hand, newspaper headlines and editorials that predicted the complete mechanization of the cavalry and the extinction of the horse as a weapon in modern warfare outraged many traditional cavalrymen. Though it was far from a match made in heaven, both groups had no other choice for the immediate future.[22]

Though MacArthur disbanded the Mechanized Force, he did not prohibit other branches from using new technology when and where possible. In fact, he promoted the notion of modernization throughout the Army. The National Defense Act of 1920 directed that tanks remain the express responsibility of the infantry. To circumvent this restriction, the "combat car" became the responsibility of the cavalry. The "combat car" was a mechanized vehicle capable of fast cross-country travel in support of, or independent of, horse cavalry.[23] In reality, "combat cars" and tanks were usually identical. Indeed, during the 1930s, the cavalry and infantry often used identical vehicles, which were merely given different official designations. Arguably, MacArthur was one of the most forward-looking senior officers in the Army during this period. He realized that, although the money was then unavailable for full modernization, every effort was needed

On July 28, 1932, U.S. Army Chief of Staff General Douglas MacArthur directed the controversial eviction of the so-called "Bonus Army" from its makeshift camp in Washington, D.C. (*LOC*)

FT17 tank chassis in 1922. (*LOC*)

to make improvements where possible. As far as the cavalry was concerned, MacArthur foresaw its complete reorganization.[24]

In November 1931, the cavalry officers and enlisted men of the Mechanized Force transferred to Fort Knox, Kentucky, where they eventually formed a mechanized cavalry regiment. The remainder of the Mechanized Force personnel, however, transferred back to their original branches. The War Department designated Van Voorhis and Adna R. Chaffee, Jr., a cavalryman and General Staff officer who had never been inside a tank, as the mechanized cavalry regiment's commander and executive officer, respectively. Chaffee, described as both one of the best horsemen and one of the "best brains" in the Army, was profoundly influenced by his experiences in World War I and abandoned horse cavalry, both literally and conceptually, soon thereafter. Van Voorhis and Chaffee arrived at Fort Knox to find a dilapidated World War I post, which only the Kentucky National Guard and college ROTC detachments used during the intervening dozen years. It was not until after the inauguration of President Franklin D. Roosevelt that millions of dollars from the newly organized Public Works Administration were used to rehabilitate and expand of Fort Knox.[25] It would take two more years before both a regiment and the soldiers to fill that regiment arrived at Fort Knox. Rather than dismounting an existing horse regiment in order to furnish the men to create the mechanized regiment, the general feeling in the cavalry branch was that it would be a better idea to stand up a deactivated regiment (15th, 16th, or 17th Cavalry Regiments) and recruit new men to fill its ranks.[26]

Throughout the 1930s, Van Voorhis, Chaffee, and other cavalry officers worked to develop and expand mechanized cavalry. In March 1932, even before the Army chose a regiment to transfer to Fort Knox, the War Department designated the post as the home of the 7th Cavalry Brigade (Mechanized). The Chief of Cavalry, Major General Guy V. Henry, Jr., also informed Van Voorhis and Chaffee that as soon as they finished training their first mechanized cavalry regiment, a second regiment would be added to the brigade. Despite these assurances, however, a political battle erupted over which state (and therefore which congressman and senators) would lose a cavalry regiment in order to furnish the regiment for Fort Knox.[27] Finally, the War Department chose the 1st Cavalry Regiment for transfer to Fort Knox, where it joined the remnants of the Mechanized Force. However, many of the officers and enlisted men of the 1st Cavalry were far from happy with their assignment. When leaving Fort D. A. Russell in Marfa, Texas, many of the officers and enlisted men of the 1st Cavalry performed ceremonies more akin to "funeral services" than any traditional Army change of post or change of command ceremonies. Major Robert W. Grow, the S-3 (Operations and Training) for the Mechanized Force and later also for the 1st Cavalry, reported that most of the enlisted men of the 1st Cavalry were "interested and welcomed the change" from horses. Most of the officers, however, were "doubtful [and] showed more interest in their future assignments with horse units."[28]

Throughout 1933, the 1st Cavalry reorganized and trained in mechanized warfare, which was a learning experience for all concerned, because a completely mechanized regiment was new to the U.S. Army. Finally, in May 1934, the 1st Cavalry Regiment (Mechanized) participated in maneuvers at Fort Riley to test mechanized cavalry both in support of and against horse cavalry. Two horse cavalry regiments, the 2nd and 13th Cavalry, formed a provisional brigade to counter the 1st Cavalry during a portion of the maneuvers. The maneuvers took on two basic forms: exercises in which horse and mechanized units fought against each other and those in which the units fought alongside one another against other horse units.[29] Van Voorhis was unable to participate in these historic maneuvers because he had been transferred to Schofield Barracks where he served as the Chief of Staff of the Hawaiian Department, and Chaffee served as temporary commander of the 1st Cavalry.

The results of the maneuvers, as presented in the *Cavalry Journal*, downplayed any accomplishments of the 1st Cavalry and emphasized only mechanized cavalry's limitations. Almost no negative comments were made about horse cavalry and the overall conclusion seemed to be that mechanization gave more versatility to the horse cavalry.[30] In actuality, the maneuvers displayed the significant advantages of mechanized cavalry as well as the increased vulnerability of horse cavalry formations on the modern battlefield. Chaffee barely contained his anger at the "official" version of events.

> They seem blind to the possibilities of a mechanized cavalry. Those fellows at Riley ought to understand that the definition of cavalry now includes troops of any kind

On April 6, 1938, President Franklin D. Roosevelt reviewed the Army Day Parade on the anniversary of America's entry into World War I. The M2A2 tank in the photo belonged to Company A, 66th Infantry Regiment (Light Tanks).
Left to right: Brigadier General William F. Bryan; Roosevelt; Brigadier General Albert Cox, commander of the 155th Field Artillery Brigade; and Assistant Secretary of War Louis Johnson. (*LOC*)

FT17 tank undergoing an engine overhaul, 1925. (*LOC*)

Cavalry officer-student at the Cavalry School, Fort Riley, Kansas, demonstrates the amazing agility of a well-trained cavalry horse, *c.* 1921. (*USCM*)

> equipped for highly mobile combat and not just mounted on horses. The motto of the [Cavalry] School says, "Through Mobility We Conquer." It does not say, "Through Mobility on Horses Alone We Conquer."[31]

Grow believed that the performance of the 1st Cavalry impressed most junior officers, but that senior officers seemed unable to "sense the inevitable."[32] As a result, mechanized cavalry continued to labor under many constraints. For example, on May 1, 1935, the 1st Cavalry had a total of sixty-five combat cars, armored cars, scout cars, and personnel carriers, but they included ten designs from four different manufacturers.[33] This lack of standardization made it difficult to evaluate mechanized cavalry's potential for future success.

In the late summer of 1936, the 7th Cavalry Brigade participated in the Second Army Maneuvers at Fort Knox and Camp Custer, Michigan. These maneuvers were the first time that mechanized cavalry was both supported and opposed by infantry, horse cavalry, and artillery. During the maneuvers, the 7th Cavalry Brigade was augmented by a battalion of motorized artillery from the 19th Field Artillery Regiment and two temporarily motorized battalions of the 201st Infantry Regiment (West Virginia National Guard). During the first phase of the maneuvers, held at Fort Knox, the 7th Cavalry Brigade was ordered to delay an advancing infantry corps and horse cavalry brigade. Not only did the brigade

Troopers from the 2nd Cavalry Regiment in the chow line while on maneuvers. (*USCM*)

Members of the 2nd Cavalry Regiment make camp while on maneuvers. (*USCM*)

succeed in delaying the enemy formations, it also overran several of the enemy's infantry battalions. The second phase of the maneuvers, held at Camp Custer, produced largely the same results as the first, though the 7th Cavalry Brigade was saddled during this phase with horse cavalry and foot infantry, which limited its effectiveness.[34]

The results of the maneuvers prompted several recommendations by Colonel Bruce Palmer, then the commander the 1st Cavalry Regiment, regarding the organization and equipment of the 7th Cavalry Brigade. The artillery battalion performed so well that Palmer believed it should be a permanent part of the 7th Cavalry Brigade. The two motorized infantry battalions also performed very well, but Palmer, while praising their performance, was careful not to request the permanent presence of infantrymen, which might ignite accusations that he was trying to recreate the Mechanized Force. Instead, he recommended that a rifle troop be included in each mechanized cavalry regiment to perform many of the duties of the motorized infantry. Palmer also noted that all of the units involved in the maneuvers were desperately short of anti-tank weapons, which he thought might have negated some of the 7th Cavalry Brigade's accomplishments. Finally, he argued that the 7th Cavalry Brigade needed quartermaster and ordnance troops at the brigade level to provide logistics and maintenance support.[35]

After the maneuvers, Van Voorhis, who had returned to command the 7th Cavalry Brigade, made it his first priority to secure another cavalry regiment to augment the brigade. The regiment most frequently mentioned for this purpose was the 4th Cavalry, stationed at Fort Meade, South Dakota. Its remote location meant that it had played little or no role in national defense, which made it ideal for transfer to Fort Knox. However, the congressman in whose district Fort Meade was located absolutely refused to agree to the plan and received sufficient support from his colleagues to block the move.[36] Unable to secure the 4th Cavalry, Van Voorhis and Major General Leon B. Kromer, the new Chief of Cavalry, suggested reactivating the 15th Cavalry Regiment, which required the existing horse cavalry regiments to contribute only a small cadre of officers and enlisted men. The remainder of the troopers would be recruited from civilian life, a process made easier by the fact that many former soldiers were unemployed as a result of the Great Depression. While this proposal seemed to be the perfect compromise, Congress refused to appropriate the funds.[37] Not until 1938 did Van Voorhis' vision of a complete mechanized cavalry brigade come to fruition. In early 1938, the 7th Cavalry Brigade was expanded with the 13th Cavalry and 68th Field Artillery regiments.

By the late 1930s, most cavalry officers began to recognize the important role that mechanized forces would play in any future war, though many were, as yet, unwilling to abandon the horse as an instrument of warfare. The proposed solution to the problem of how to coordinate both horse and mechanized cavalry was the formation of the horse-mechanized regiment. The horse-mechanized regiment consisted of a headquarters troop, a service troop, a squadron of

End of the chow line and a hot mug of coffee. (*USCM*)

Major General John K. Herr being sworn in as Chief of Cavalry on March 26, 1938. *Left to right*: Major General Allen W. Cullion, Judge Advocate General; Herr and outgoing Chief of Cavalry Major General Leon B. Kromer. (*LOC*)

truck-borne horse cavalry, and a mechanized squadron. The cavalry branch intended to use the horse-mechanized regiment exclusively for corps-level reconnaissance.[38] The regiment was a rather awkwardly organized unit, since the horse squadron was more vulnerable, slower, and more difficult to deploy than the mechanized squadron. The concept ultimately proved so unsuccessful that the two Regular Army (4th and 6th Cavalry Regiments) and seven National Guard (101st, 102nd, 104th, 106th, 107th, 113th, and 115th Cavalry Regiments) horse-mechanized regiments were completely mechanized and reorganized during World War II.[39]

In August 1939, the First Army held maneuvers in the vicinity of the Plattsburg, New York, which essentially pitted the Regular Army against the National Guard. During the maneuvers, four National Guard infantry divisions (26th (Massachusetts), 27th (New York), 43rd (Connecticut, Maine, Rhode Island, and Vermont), and 44th (Delaware, New Jersey, and New York)), a cavalry regiment (101st Cavalry Regiment—New York National Guard), and a tank battalion (66th Infantry Regiment—Light Tanks) faced one Regular Army infantry division

Cavalrymen of one of the "Horse-Mechanized" regiments load their horses on trailers for transportation, *c.* 1939. (*USCM*)

(1st Infantry Division), an infantry brigade (18th Infantry Brigade of the 9th Infantry Division), and the 7th Cavalry Brigade.[40] For the 7th Cavalry, these maneuvers presented the opportunity to perform independent mechanized action over diverse terrain and to demonstrate their abilities to a skeptical audience. The brigade performed far beyond expectations and surprised many Army officers who had no experience with mechanized units. Chaffee noted that in order to protect against mechanized attack during the maneuvers, the opposing force used as much as 50 percent of their artillery in an anti-tank role, which diminished their ability to provide traditional artillery support. At one point, the brigade was halted since it was about to overrun the rear area of the opposing force and, therefore, prematurely end the maneuvers.[41]

The month after the First Army maneuvers, German mechanized forces overwhelmed the horse cavalry of Poland. Unfortunately, those European developments were still not enough to convince the most skeptical U.S. Army officers of the utility of mechanization. Therefore, in October 1939, the 1st Cavalry Division staged a series of maneuvers in Texas. The 1st Cavalry Division was horse-mounted and retained the older "square" division structure of two brigades, each with two regiments.[42] The maneuvers were divided into four phases—two of which generated interesting results regarding mechanization. Phase II of the maneuvers began with the division's two brigades separated by approximately 45 miles. The area of contact contained an important hill and this geographic feature caught the attention of both brigades. Since the 2nd Cavalry Brigade contained an armored car detachment, its troops were the first to reach the hill and hold it until reinforced by the remainder of the brigade. As a result, the 2nd Cavalry Brigade ultimately won the "battle" of Phase II.[43]

Phase IV of the maneuvers found the entire 1st Cavalry Division operating against an *ad hoc* motorized infantry formation consisting of the 9th Infantry Regiment and a battalion of truck-drawn artillery. The 9th Infantry actually put the 1st Cavalry Division on the defensive for part of the maneuvers and though the infantry lost a third of its combat power "in action" (3rd Battalion was ruled destroyed), the regiment was still able to regroup and was in defensive positions under attack by the entire 1st Cavalry Division when the maneuvers ended. The results of this phase and of the maneuvers as a whole reaffirmed some of the results of the First Army Maneuvers. The most important conclusions drawn from the 1st Cavalry Division exercises were that mounted horse cavalry attacks against modern infantry were "suicidal" and that armored cars completely usurped the reconnaissance role from horses.[44]

In May 1940, the final act in the drama over mechanized cavalry occurred immediately after the Third Army Maneuvers in Louisiana. During the maneuvers, the IX Corps with the 7th Cavalry Brigade was opposed by the IV Corps with the infantry's Provisional Tank Brigade (commanded by Brigadier General Bruce Magruder, the most senior infantry tanker).[45] The first phase of the maneuvers involved these larger forces engaging one another as had occurred in earlier

M2A2 tank from Company B, 66th Infantry Regiment (Light Tanks) during the 1938 Army Day Parade. (*LOC*)

Trooper from the 2nd Cavalry Regiment takes a nap after lunch while on maneuvers. (*USCM*)

Scout cars and a truck of the 2nd Cavalry Regiment on maneuvers, *c.* 1938. (*USCM*)

maneuvers, but the second phase was truly revolutionary. During the second phase, the 7th Cavalry Brigade was combined with the Infantry's Provisional Tank Brigade to form an *ad hoc* division—the first division-sized mechanized formation in U.S. Army history. During the last exercise of the maneuvers, the provisional mechanized division launched an attack on a prepared enemy position. The mechanized force penetrated the position and was thoroughly routing its opponents when the maneuvers ended.[46]

On May 24, 1940, the final day of the maneuvers, Chaffee, Magruder, Major General Stanley D. Embrick (commander of the Third Army), Brigadier General Frank M. Andrews (U.S. Army Assistant Chief of Staff for Operations and Training), and Patton (now a full colonel and an umpire at the maneuvers) met in the basement of the Alexandria (Louisiana) High School to discuss the future of mechanization. Significantly, neither the Chief of Cavalry nor the Chief of Infantry, both of whom attended the maneuvers, were invited to this impromptu conference. All of the conference participants agreed that, if mechanization were to succeed in the Army, it had to be taken out of the hands of the cavalry and infantry. In the opinion of the participants, both the cavalry and infantry branches continued to view mechanization as only an auxiliary to their existing forces, rather than as a revolutionary new weapon.[47] The original decision to allow the cavalry and infantry to develop different mechanized vehicles was based on the idea that weapons needed to fit doctrine, rather than the other way around. By

1940, the supporters of mechanization believed that while mechanized doctrine and vehicles evolved during the interwar period in other nations, the opponents of mechanization prevented a similar evolution in the U.S. Army.

When the conference ended, Andrews returned to Washington to present the recommendations to the U.S. Army Chief of Staff, General George C. Marshall. As a result, a second and more formal conference was held in Washington on June 10, 1940, which involved most of the original participants, along with the Chiefs of Cavalry and Infantry. For several hours, the branch chiefs argued they were the proper individuals to develop mechanized forces, but their lack of progress on the issue ultimately betrayed them. The conference ended without any formal decision, but within two weeks, Marshall, on the advice of Andrews and others, had made his choice. On June 24, 1940, Marshall announced his decision to create a separate Armored Force with Chaffee as its first chief.[48]

During the interwar period, mechanization was the most important issue in the U.S. Cavalry. One of the most significant problems for the cavalry regarding mechanization was a lack of funding. Without major expenditures on an annual basis, the cavalry was unable to procure the cutting-edge technology necessary to produce a truly viable mechanized force. In addition to a lack of funding, the state

The Color Guard of 3rd Cavalry Regiment, wearing 1880s-period uniforms, Fort Myers, Virginia, *c.* 1927. (*USCM*)

of technological development during this period also played a role in decisions. Indeed, it was not until the late 1920s, with the Model 1928 Christie tank, that a significant technological innovation occurred in armored fighting vehicle design. However, inspired leadership was the single most important factor necessary to mechanize the cavalry and it was often sorely lacking at crucial points. Only the efforts of a small group of individuals kept mechanization alive during the interwar Army.

3

"Traditionalists": Proponents of the Horse

Mechanizing the interwar U.S. Cavalry was an intellectual rather than a physical battle. Officers held different views regarding the ideal composition, organization, and even the culture of future cavalry forces. The discussion of these issues took place in officers' clubs, lectures at the Command and General Staff School (CGSS) or the Army War College, in personal correspondence, and in the pages of the cavalry branch's professional publication—the *Cavalry Journal.* While some officers threw their support behind developing technology, others, who could accurately be termed "traditionalists," vehemently supported the horse and the socio-cultural stability that it represented. The most prominent, both by their ranks and the important assignments they occupied, of these horse cavalry supporters were Major General John K. Herr and Brigadier General Hamilton S. Hawkins. They both supported the horse and opposed mechanization at every opportunity, which hampered the mechanization process since they occupied positions of senior authority within the small general officer corps of the period. Ultimately, Herr and Hawkins demonstrated that their support was based on nothing more than traditionalism in both sentiment and culture.

Hamilton S. Hawkins was born at Fort Yellowstone, North Dakota, on September 25, 1872. The son of Brigadier General Hamilton S. Hawkins, he graduated from the U.S. Military Academy, West Point, New York, in 1894. After service with the 4th Cavalry Regiment during the Philippine Insurrection, he served as an instructor of mathematics at West Point. Hawkins graduated from the School of the Line in 1911, followed by the Army Staff College in 1912.[1] He then served on exchange with the 6th Dragoons of the French Army and afterward the 2nd Brandenburg Dragoons of the Imperial Germany Army. After the outbreak of World War I, Hawkins served on various staffs until June 1918, when he deployed to France with the 35th Division—where he served as the division Chief of Staff and later the acting commander of the 69th Infantry Brigade.[2] During the interwar period, Hawkins, by then a colonel, served in a series of senior cavalry positions, ending his career as a brigadier general and the commander of the 1st Cavalry Division at Fort Bliss, Texas.[3]

Colonel Hamilton S. Hawkins in April 1923. (*LOC*)

After the decision to "recreate" the Mechanized Force in 1930, Hawkins began a crusade in support of the horse, primarily in the pages of the *Cavalry Journal*, which lasted until the end of World War II. His reactions to the inclusion of mechanized units within the Cavalry were riddled with inconsistencies, revealing a loyalty to horses based on personal bias rather than technological and other empirical evidence. For example, in 1931, Hawkins wrote an article to denounce what he saw as rumor-mongering in the popular press regarding mechanization in the cavalry. His chief objection was that the organization of the "permanent" and independent Mechanized Force caused many Americans to think that the horse was doomed to be replaced by the machine. Though Hawkins believed that mechanization would be valuable in future warfare, he argued that mechanized vehicles could not operate in every kind of terrain. In fact, he thought that mechanized vehicles were useful only for "smaller and less important missions."[4] While Hawkins' beliefs were in accordance with the then current Army policy, he went a step further by saying:

> There is an idea prevailing among some officers that the Mechanized Force is to be assigned Cavalry missions in what is termed ordinary country, and Cavalry kept for work in [a] difficult country. This idea is very false and dangerous.[5]

Interestingly, despite these assertions, he was directly contradicting the mechanization directive issued by the new Chief of Staff, General Douglas MacArthur.

Brigadier General Douglas MacArthur seated in the original chair of the old lord of St. Benoit Chateau, France, 1918. (*NARA*)

Hawkins' other comments further revealed contradictory arguments and a lack of understanding regarding mechanized technology. Hawkins admitted that he had seen demonstrations of tanks knocking down trees and stone walls, but he thought it was "absurd to think of tanks and passenger trucks, carrying machine gunners, romping through the woods and swamps, creeks and villages at the speed that Cavalry can attain."[6] Despite this assertion, in the very next paragraph of the article, Hawkins criticized mechanized forces for moving too fast on the battlefield. He stated that it was the job of cavalry to fight in conjunction with and support of infantry, "Not to precede the Infantry by a hundred miles."[7] Hawkins' contradictory comments in these two paragraphs demonstrate his confusion on the topic of mechanization. Either mechanized vehicles were capable of fast, cross-country travel, or they were not. Hawkins oddly believed that they were too slow in circumstances when they should have moved faster and *vice versa*.

Another of Hawkins' arguments was based on his belief that increased mobility was of little use, since all soldiers (artillery, cavalry, and infantry) were transported over long distances to the site of a battle. The problem with his argument was that it presupposed set-piece battles, such as those in World War I, where the site of the battle had already been established and both sides had time to prepare for the battle. Therefore, Hawkins appeared to be unable to conceive of large-scale mobile warfare, where the site of the battle was wherever the two opposing armies came into contact. In addition, he believed that mechanized forces only advanced rapidly over roads and that they were no faster than foot infantry over unpaved

Cavalry performing field drills in 1919. (*NARA*)

surfaces.[8] Hawkins' opinion of mechanized vehicles was undoubtedly the result of his service during World War I, a conclusion supported by his comments later on in the article. Apparently, he was unaware of, or refused to acknowledge, the evolution that mechanized vehicles had undergone since the end of World War I.

The apparent inconsistencies of Hawkins' article continued when he took umbrage with the outdated belief that modern cavalry initiated mounted charges against enemy positions. Correctly, he pointed out that the cavalry had not performed saber charges since well before the Spanish-American War, but rather dismounted and engaged the enemy with small arms. Yet, later in the article, Hawkins stated that some officers wrongly saw the cavalry as "only a mounted Infantry using horses merely to increase its mobility."[9] Despite the changes in cavalry roles, horse cavalry continued to perform mounted reconnaissance against enemy flanks and Hawkins acknowledged that mechanized vehicles might help to prevent this reconnaissance by enemy horse cavalry. Nevertheless, he also asserted that mechanized vehicles were incapable of performing reconnaissance. Somehow it was possible that mechanized forces were capable of counter-reconnaissance, but not of the reconnaissance itself. The vulnerability of tanks to artillery was yet another of Hawkins' complaints about mechanized vehicles.[10] Yet horses and men were vulnerable to small arms as well as artillery.

The decision to integrate the Mechanized Force into the cavalry as the 1st Cavalry Regiment (Mechanized) must have mollified Hawkins, because his articles did not appear in the pages of the *Cavalry Journal* for several years. Nevertheless, his next documented response to mechanization demonstrated a state of denial rather than any attempt at true argument. While serving as the commander of the 1st Cavalry Division in 1935, Hawkins responded to a memorandum forwarded to him by the Cavalry Board at Fort Riley. The Cavalry Board asked specific questions regarding the methods of divisional reorganization resulting in a more mobile structure. Hawkins rather dismissively referred to the 1st Cavalry Regiment (Mechanized) as the "mechanized force" and refused to acknowledge that cavalry meant anything other than men mounted on horses:

> Mechanized forces may assist but cannot replace cavalry on these cross country missions, because, in spite of unproven assertions that large numbers of mechanized forces can travel speedily across country, no reliance can be based upon these assertions. And, even though they were true, the rapid development in anti-tank weapons and armor-piercing bullets would make it extremely hazardous to put faith in a new organization of this kind for the accomplishment of great cavalry missions.[11]

Hawkins refused to acknowledge the results of several Army maneuvers that had proved the ability of mechanized cavalry to travel cross-country. In addition, he again noted the vulnerability of mechanized vehicles but made no reference to the far greater vulnerability of horses and men. Hawkins went on to state that "mobility of a cavalry division cannot be increased," which illustrated his inability to see cavalry as anything other than men mounted on horses.[12] Despite his

Troopers and horses of the 107th Cavalry Regiment (Ohio National Guard). This photo does a good job of demonstrating the less glamorous aspects of being a cavalryman! (*USCM*)

apparent disregard for motor vehicles, he recommended that the quartermaster company of each division should be completely mechanized. The closing sentence of Hawkins' memorandum speaks volumes about his opinions. "It would be easy to overdo the ... mechanization of the Army."[13]

After his retirement in 1936, Hawkins continued to refuse to both acknowledge the significance technological advances of mechanical vehicles or the limitations of the horse. He used the conflicts in Spain, China, and North Africa as examples of the inability of mechanized vehicles to perform at the levels that their supporters had prophesied. Hawkins believed that horse cavalry continued to be as effective in combat as it had always been, especially in open warfare with no trenches or barbed-wire entanglements. "Tanks, light or heavy, have a special task to support the infantry, but they can never be either numerous or effective enough to replace cavalry."[14] Unfortunately, the conflicts he mentioned were fought by second- or third-rate powers, who did not have the industrial and manufacturing capacity of the United States or the major powers of Europe.

Interestingly, it was not until 1937 that Hawkins finally began to recognize that technological developments had markedly changed the effectiveness of tanks. His solution was to advocate the use of cavalry in support of tanks, much in the same way that infantry had been used to support tanks in World War I. The cavalry, Hawkins argued, could keep up with the tanks more easily and cheaply than infantry, since the infantry would have to be motorized if it were to keep up with the tanks.[15] Nevertheless, Hawkins continued to point out the shortcomings of the tank:

> The light tank cannot move cross-country on all kinds of ground with the celerity of cavalry. While moving to attack, the guns in the tanks cannot fire with accuracy, and if they halt to shoot, they are too easily hit by fire of anti-tank machine guns and cannon.[16]

Again, Hawkins pointed out weaknesses in mechanized vehicles but refused to acknowledge that horses and men are even more prone to these same weaknesses. He also claimed that the "operation of tanks exhausts their crews very soon in any extended operations."[17] This assertion was curious because it implied that somehow infantry and cavalry were less exhausted by combat than tankers.

Hawkins continued his discussion of mechanized vehicle shortcomings when he discussed the thickness of their armor. "Light tanks cannot be armored by more than a half inch of steel armor plate, if that much."[18] While that was true at the time the article was written, Hawkins was precluding the possibility of innovations that allowed for armor thickness to increase. Hawkins urged caution in changing horse cavalry to mechanized vehicles as the Europeans were then in the process of doing. "European armies are likely to find out that they have made a serious error in going blindly so far."[19] As far as American mechanization was concerned, he believed that "when the tests of war have made the facts clear, we shall certainly regret having tried to replace cavalry with mechanization."[20] Hawkins irrational arguments suggest that his distaste for mechanized vehicles was based not in fact, but primarily in emotion.

In a 1938 article, Hawkins discussed European developments and accused the principal European powers of a "lack of imagination or imagination gone wild" and a "sheep-like rush to mechanization."[21] Hawkins referred to their mechanized cavalry units as "so-called cavalry," which again suggests that he was incapable of believing that cavalry could exist without horses. The role of cavalry on the modern battlefield was one of the main points of this article. Despite the lessons of World War I, Hawkins dismissed the notion that reconnaissance was to be the principal role of the cavalry in the future. His vision was fixed on the role of cavalry during the American Civil War, particularly Brigadier General John Buford's delaying action at the Battle of Gettysburg. Despite this desire for the cavalry to have a role other than reconnaissance, Hawkins rejected the use of the light machine gun (Browning Automatic Rifle), which was perfectly suited for this role.[22] In addition, Hawkins believed that there were "too many" machine guns attached to horse cavalry units, which he thought slowed them down considerably.[23] Only a year after saying that armor plating could not go beyond half an inch, he noted that some tanks now boasted an inch of armor plating. Hawkins saw no problem in this, because he believed that as armor got thicker, the vehicle got slower and therefore be of no threat in anything other than trench warfare.[24] He made this assertion despite the fact that mechanized vehicles were then actually increasing in speed as new and more powerful engines were developed. Hawkins continued to ignore technological developments in favor of his own emotional bias—in the case of the European situation, a bias reinforced by jingoistic nationalism.

NCO Club, 8th Cavalry Regiment, 1939. The club's sign says: "Let no one cross this threshold hence. And report things said in confidence." (*USCM*)

German military *attaché* Lieutenant General Friedrich von Bötticher visiting the Cavalry School at Fort Riley, Kansas, *c*. 1936. (*USCM*)

In his regular column in the *Cavalry Journal*, Hawkins continued to criticize Europe's decision to downplay the horse. In 1940, he discussed the early phases of the German campaign in France. Hawkins began his column by stating that nothing up to that point (May 20, 1940) in World War II had disproved his continued statements regarding the horse in modern warfare. He greatly criticized the French for relying far too heavily on static defenses, such as the Maginot Line. Hawkins criticized the British for permitting "such pseudo military experts as Liddell Hart and others to influence the military principles under which they were arming, organizing, and training."[25] Britain and France were also criticized for their decision to abandon the horse, and he made much of the fact that their failures were, in his opinion, primarily due to this decision. Even the Germans were criticized, because they "may find that despite their success so far, they need cavalry to make good the penetrations in an enemy's line accomplished by their mechanized forces."[26] Thus, despite the overwhelming successes of mechanized forces in Poland in 1939 and in France in 1940, Hawkins continued to refuse to acknowledge these achievements.

Throughout World War II, Hawkins continued to write extensively about the need for horse cavalry in terrain such as that of the Philippines, where he believed mechanized forces were relatively useless. He castigated Britain, France, and the Soviet Union for neglecting their horse cavalry, which was, in his opinion, the cause of their defeats by the Germans. The German victories without horse cavalry were excused away as the result of "having beaten her unprepared enemies with overwhelming forces."[27] Hawkins made his prejudices clear by saying that though cavalry formations should have a few mechanized vehicles, "primarily a cavalry unit is composed of horsemen" and that "those cavalrymen who have been transferred to the Armored Forces are no longer cavalrymen."[28] Unrepentant to the end, he noted in his last regular column soon after the war: "The fact that military successes in our army [occurred] without the use of horse cavalry does not alter in the least my opinion that such cavalry in large numbers could have been used to great advantage in tactical operations which would have saved both time and losses."[29] Therefore, Hawkins ultimately admitted that his advocacy of the horse was a matter of faith and not of empirical evidence.

The other main cavalry "traditionalist," John K. Herr, was also born into a prominent military family, and rose to an elite position in the cavalry shortly after Hawkins' retirement. Born in White House, New Jersey, on October 1, 1878, Herr graduated from West Point in 1902. His early career followed a relatively ordinary path, including field service and an instructorship at West Point. During World War I, he was the Chief of Staff of the 30th Division in France from June 1918 to April 1919.[30] From January 1921 to January 1922, Herr served as the Assistant Chief of Staff for Operations (G-3) and then the Assistant Chief of Staff for Logistics (G-4) for the American Forces in Germany.[31] Throughout the 1920s and 1930s, Herr served in command positions in the cavalry along with a few detours for education.[32] Herr's last assignment before

Major General Malin Craig, Chief of Cavalry, June 26, 1924. (*LOC*)

his promotion to Chief of Cavalry in 1938 was command of the 7th Cavalry Regiment. Interestingly, Herr's selection as Chief of Cavalry appears to have been based on his longtime friendship with the U.S. Army Chief of Staff, Malin Craig, rather than his pro-horse sentiments. Craig was not anti-mechanization either during his tenure as Chief of Cavalry between 1924 and 1926 or as Chief of Staff and supported the previous Chief of Cavalry, Leon B. Kromer, in his pro-mechanization decisions.

As Chief of Cavalry until 1942, Herr quickly demonstrated his commitment to horse cavalry in spite of the superiority of mechanized forces. For example, in a memorandum prepared for the Adjutant General of the U.S. Army in 1938, Herr admitted that mechanized cavalry possessed superior firepower, shock, and strategic and tactical mobility than horse cavalry. Herr also noted that mechanized cavalry was more sensitive to terrain and had less capacity for sustained independent action than horse cavalry.[33] Still, despite these rather significant acknowledgments and the recommendation that additional motor vehicles be purchased for the cavalry, he advised the Adjutant General that only one additional mechanized cavalry regiment should be formed and that in the National Guard.[34] Although aware of mechanization's benefits, Herr chose to give mechanized forces only token representation in the cavalry, which he determined would continue to be dominated by horses.

Herr's faith in the horse rested mainly on his reverence for American military tradition. According to Herr, the European horse cavalry was ineffective against mechanized forces due primarily, not to the horse's obsolescence, but to the lack of preparation on the part of the Europeans. He believed that this, naturally, was not the case with the American military, which he stated had refined horse warfare to an art since the Civil War. Responding to pro-mechanization critics, Herr also pointed to the fact that Poland and the Soviet Union maintained large formations of horse cavalry, and emphasized his inclusion of mechanized forces in the cavalry as evidence of open-mindedness. In short, Herr based his advocacy of the horse on his belief in America's historical cavalry traditions and specific capabilities mentioned above, rather than on any empirical evidence such as the German success in Poland and France.

In 1938, the War Department requested that both the Office of the Chief of Cavalry and the 7th Cavalry Brigade (Mechanized) submit a plan for the creation of a mechanized cavalry division. The idea of a mechanized cavalry division had been discussed for years, but this was the first official inquiry into the possibility of forming such a division. Though Herr officially approved the resulting division organization, he privately disliked the idea of a mechanized cavalry division and did whatever he could to sabotage it. To Major Robert W. Grow, a "modernizer" who was then serving in the Office of the Chief of Cavalry, Herr stated that the War Department would "take a single horse soldier away over his dead body."[35] Additionally, Herr wanted to break up the 7th Cavalry Brigade by sending one of its regiments to Fort Riley or by sending the entire brigade down to the Mexican border, where he believed it was of more use to national defense.[36] Either of these actions would have made it difficult or impossible to continue the development of mechanized cavalry doctrine.

In the *Cavalry Journal* in early 1939, Herr discussed the future of cavalry in light of international developments. He began by citing many of the same examples previously mentioned by Hawkins. Herr used the American Civil War and World War I as examples of the success or failure to use horse cavalry properly. He then stated that only the Polish and Soviet armies understood the proper use of horse cavalry and retained sufficiently large bodies of horse-mounted soldiers. Herr cautioned that "any independent body of troops that expects to rely solely upon [mechanized] vehicles of any kind for an adequate ground reconnaissance under all conditions is courting disaster."[37] This demonstrated Herr's rather poor understanding of the military situations in Poland and the Soviet Union. The Poles, for instance, wished to mechanize far larger portions of their cavalry (only one Polish cavalry regiment had been fully mechanized by September 1939), but lacked both the funds and the industrial base to do so.[38] The most important point about Herr's assertions was that he published the article in the same year that the mechanized forces of Germany overran the horse cavalry of Poland.

At the same time this article appeared, Herr repeated his arguments regarding the limitations of mechanized forces before the Military Affairs Subcommittee of the Committee on Appropriations in the U.S. House of Representatives. Uncharacteristically, he began his remarks to the subcommittee by touting the development of mechanized cavalry:

> Our studies and experiments have convinced us that we can apply automotive machines to the execution of cavalry missions to a very considerable extent. We are satisfied that the iron horse is here to stay.[39]

Nevertheless, Herr also believed that mechanized cavalry should only exist as a small portion of the cavalry branch and that it was most effective in co-operation with horse cavalry. When a congressman asked him whether or not he envisioned the complete mechanization of the cavalry, Herr replied: "The answer is distinctly no. No vehicle can go over the difficult country that a horse can."[40] Another congressman challenged Herr's defense of horse cavalry by saying, "You do not mean to state that you are going to lead a Charge of the Light Brigade in the face of the modern machine gun?"[41] Herr denied that possibility, but was unable to convince the congressmen that horse cavalry was still effective in the face of modern weaponry, especially as a result of the lack of use of horse cavalry in World War I.

In spite of Herr's distrust of mechanization, he preferred to maintain mechanized vehicles under his command, subordinate to horse cavalry, rather than to allow mechanized forces to become a separate branch within the Army. In this context in 1939, Herr wrote to Brigadier General Adna R. Chaffee, Jr., then the commander of the 7th Cavalry Brigade (Mechanized) at Fort Knox, Kentucky. Herr informed Chaffee that the projected plans for the expansion

Colonel John K. Herr, commander of the 7th Cavalry Regiment, 1938. (*USCM*)

Guard Detail, Troop E, 8th Cavalry Regiment, Fort Bliss, Texas, 1926. (*USCM*)

of the mechanized cavalry brigade into a division had been disapproved by the Chief of Staff, General George C. Marshall. Not surprisingly, Chaffee was not told that part of the reason for Marshall's decision rested on Herr's intransigence and refusal to allow any horse cavalry regiments to be mechanized. Nevertheless, Chaffee had already been informed of Herr's efforts by colleagues in the War Department. Herr told Chaffee that despite the decision not to expand the brigade, money had still been appropriated for brigade improvements. The brigade was to be improved by the expansion of the brigade headquarters troop, the addition of a third squadron to the 1st and 13th Cavalry Regiments, and the addition of several motorcycle formations.[42] While the first two points were indeed improvements, the addition of motorcycles was viewed by most mechanized cavalry officers as a hindrance. Herr wanted to replace many of the "combat cars" with motorcycles, which mechanized cavalry officers believed limited the combat firepower of the mechanized cavalry and made them more vulnerable to attack (since a motorcycle was more vulnerable to small arms than a "combat car"/tank was). Herr concluded his letter by mentioning that there had been some talk "unofficially, about the desirability of organizing a [new and independent] mechanized force."[43] Clearly, Herr was disturbed by this possibility and was trying to placate, with the projected improvements, the most likely commander of any such force—namely Chaffee.

Though Herr consistently refused to compromise on horse cavalry, the German invasion of Poland changed Herr's attitude toward Chaffee somewhat. "[Herr] is afraid of Chaffee, afraid Chaffee will take advantage of the looked for expansion of mechanization to go for a separate corps."[44] Despite this attitude, little progress was made toward the creation of the mechanized cavalry division during the remainder of 1939. If Herr was indeed afraid of Chaffee, his loyalty to horse cavalry was still a more powerful motivating factor.

Two weeks after the German invasion of Poland in September 1939, Chaffee wrote a detailed memorandum to the Adjutant General, which he routed through Major General Daniel Van Voorhis, who was then the V Corps commander and Chaffee's immediate superior, on the expansion of mechanized cavalry for future warfare. Emboldened by the recent performance of mechanized units both in training and in foreign combat, Chaffee no longer couched his opinions:

> It is my belief also, based upon maneuvers and the war reports, that in any important war involving armies, and fought in a terrain where important wars are fought, mechanized cavalry is a vastly more powerful, mobile and decisive force than an equal or greater force of horse cavalry.[45]

He then blamed resistance to the expansion of the 7th Cavalry Brigade on individuals (though without mentioning any names) within the War Department who were resistant to the concept of mechanized warfare. Chaffee also provided a detailed list of recommendations, which included approval of the mechanized cavalry division organization that had already been submitted and providing

Private Ken Claydon, 121st Cavalry Regiment (New York National Guard), 1939. (*USCM*)

sufficient officers and enlisted men from existing Regular Army cavalry regiments for the formation of the division.[46]

Van Voorhis, in his capacity as Chaffee's immediate superior, endorsed Chaffee's comments completely, with the additional observation that he believed that the cavalry and infantry should continue to development mechanized forces separately because they performed different missions.[47] The Adjutant General forwarded the memorandum to Herr for his comments as the Chief of Cavalry. Herr began by agreeing with the general principles put forth in Chaffee's memorandum, but then he disagreed on several crucial points. Herr refused to allow any existing horse cavalry regiments to be used for the purpose of mechanization and he refused to release any cavalry officers or enlisted men for that purpose either. He stated that any increase in mechanized personnel should come from reserve officers, recently retired officers, National Guard personnel, and new recruits. Herr ended his comments by indirectly criticizing Chaffee for submitting the proposal directly to the Adjutant General rather than going through what he considered the proper channels by first submitting it to the Office of the Chief of Cavalry.[48] Chaffee and Herr had now publicly expressed their opinions not only about the issue of mechanization, but also concerning each other.

Cavalry 2nd Lieutenant Ronald Reagan, *c.* 1937. Reagan had volunteered for service in the Organized Reserve Corps in the 1930s because, by his own admission, the local cavalry unit had horses that he could ride for free on the weekends! (*USCM*)

In October 1939, when Grow again brought up the question of mechanization, Herr stated his position just as bluntly as he had done in the past: "Not another horseman will be dismounted."[49] Nevertheless, after both the successful use of mechanized forces during the First Army maneuvers at Plattsburg, New York, and the German invasion of Poland, Herr was forced to acknowledge that an increase in mechanized cavalry was necessary. In a three-page letter, Herr urged the immediate expansion of the 7th Cavalry Brigade into a mechanized cavalry division. He argued that it might be necessary to envision the formation of as many as four mechanized cavalry divisions if the Army expanded to the size of four field armies. Herr stressed the urgency of the necessary expansion by stating:

> When consideration is given the fact that except for a few scattered tank companies and two or three incomplete battalions, our entire army includes only one mechanized brigade, as contrasted with at least ten German armored divisions, for example, the urgency of this situation cannot be escaped.[50]

Despite these requests for expansion, Herr continued to refuse to dismount horse cavalrymen for mechanized duty. "Inasmuch as mechanization is designed to increase the scope of existing arms and not to replace them it is not considered that personnel should be provided from any existing units of any arm but should be in addition thereto."[51] Grow clearly saw what the result of this intransigence would be:

> The Chief will not reverse his stand on horse units and offer to convert any unless he can get more horse, consequently we get nothing. I will not be surprised to see a movement to take mechanization away from the Cavalry.[52]

Interestingly, only a few months later in January 1940, Herr appeared to have changed his mind regarding the accomplishments of the 7th Cavalry Brigade during the First Army maneuvers. In a letter to Brigadier General Frank M. Andrews, U.S. Army G-3, Herr complained that the terrain of the maneuvers was "entirely unsuited to the action of mechanized cavalry," despite the fact that the 7th Cavalry Brigade had distinguished itself and performed beyond expectations.[53] He then bitterly complained about the loss of experienced cavalry officers to training and schooling duties, which he believed forced the use of a National Guard horse cavalry regiment during the maneuvers. The poor performance of horse cavalry, therefore, he blamed on the poorly trained and led National Guardsmen rather than on any deficiency of horse cavalry.[54] As with Europe, Herr believed it was not the horses that were the problem, but rather poor leadership and training.

In a document that he prepared after his retirement, Herr described the last year of mechanized cavalry from his point of view. The document quotes directly from letters and memoranda that are readily available for verification, but to which he added his personal comments and opinions. In reference to the preceding letter to Marshall in October 1939, Herr commented that it was his, rather than Chaffee's,

Corporal Fuller, Los Indios, Texas, *c*. 1916. (*USCM*)

idea to propose the formation of more than one mechanized cavalry division, and that Chaffee "showed some surprise at the magnitude of the project."[55] While Chaffee may not have advocated such expansion at that moment, he had long advocated a major expansion of mechanized cavalry. In addition, former Chief of Cavalry Kromer had publicly advocated the complete mechanization of all cavalry formations.[56] Clearly, therefore, Herr could lay no legitimate claim to initiating the call for expansion of mechanized cavalry.

Herr also claimed that several officers in the War Department began "plotting to prevent the Cavalry from controlling the development [of mechanized forces]."[57] Herr stated that the Chief of Infantry, Major General George A. Lynch, told him confidentially that several infantrymen in the War Department had advised him to attempt to gain control of the Army's mechanized development. When Lynch refused to intervene, Herr stated that these same officers, with the assistance of several "traitorous" cavalry officers then serving in the office of the Chief of Staff, began to urge Marshall to form an independent mechanized force. Along with their efforts to convince Marshall, Herr stated that these same officers then began a whispering campaign against him. They stated, he believed wrongly, that he opposed mechanization in the cavalry.[58] Considering his continual refusal to dismount any further horse cavalry regiments of the purpose of mechanizing

On May 29, 1940, Senator Morris Sheppard (left), Chairman of the Senate Military Affairs Committee, Major General George A. Lynch, Chief of Infantry, and Senator A. B. Chandler of Kentucky, inspect the Johnson semi-automatic rifle, which some people at the time argued was superior to the M1 Garand. (*LOC*)

them, it would have been difficult for Marshall not to conceive of Herr as being anti-mechanization.

Herr believed that the "plotting" against him extended to the highest offices in the War Department. In a conversation, Marshall expressed his doubts about Herr's ability to handle mechanization.[59] Herr believed that these doubts were founded exclusively on the whispering campaign and poor popular press coverage. Concerning Marshall and the question of mechanization, Herr stated later:

> Never in my life have I felt more disgusted with any person. He was telling me a fighter that he doubted the expedcy [*sic.*] of appointing a man to do a job just because of a couple of untrue wisecracks.... If the Chief of Staff wished to listen to those closer to him than any Chief of Branch ever could be, that was his business and also his error.[60]

The relationship between Marshall and Herr continued to degenerate over time. Eventually, the War Department announced that the 14th Cavalry Regiment at Fort Des Moines, Iowa, was to be broken up to use its personnel to create a Reconnaissance and Support Squadron for the 7th Cavalry Brigade and an armored car squadron at Fort Riley. Herr was outraged that Marshall had made this decision because it ran completely contrary to what Herr, himself, had suggested when he was consulted on the issue.[61] After the decision had already been announced, Herr wrote to Marshall that the decision not only broke up a

Ten American copies of the French FT17 tank at Camp Merritt, New Jersey, April 12, 1918. (*NARA*)

well-trained regiment but also was contrary to the best interests of the cavalry branch.[62] Despite Herr's protests, Marshall's decision remained unchanged.

It is interesting to note the persecution complex and increasing sense of paranoia that Herr developed during the final stages of cavalry mechanization. As Chief of Cavalry, he was completely aware of the capabilities of mechanized cavalry but continually dismissed these capabilities. Marshall, as Chief of Staff, was also aware of field experiments and other developments in mechanized cavalry and had an interest in increasing the combat effectiveness of the Army for the next and, by then, inevitable war. Chaffee, as the titular head of mechanized cavalry, had a vested interest in the expansion and continued improvement of mechanization. No evidence appears to exist to support any genuine "conspiracy" against Herr by Marshall or any other officers. However, given the vested interests of both Chaffee and Marshall, it is easy to see how Herr's own fears played on his mind as both of these other men worked—independently—toward a mutual goal.

In spite of real or perceived threats, Herr continued his advocacy of horse cavalry even throughout World War II, advancing arguments based on historical continuity rather than then modern empirical evidence. In March 1940, during another appearance before the Military Affairs Subcommittee of the Committee on Appropriations, Herr was asked, "Is it not a fact that it is easier to get men with a mechanical background than it is to get good horsemen?"[63] Herr agreed that that assertion was correct, but argued that in a mechanized society such as America it was to be expected. Another congressman asked him to justify the existence of horse cavalry in light of the highly mechanized military campaigns in Europe during the previous year. Herr began, as he had done before, with a detailed exposition on the state of modern American cavalry. He then laid out a long list of the improvements made to American cavalry, including the rather curious fact that every unit in a cavalry division, except for the four combat regiments, was completely mechanized. Herr then dismissed the popular notion that modern cavalry still charged into combat with sabers or lances. Nevertheless, he also stated that "the functions of cavalry in modern war are the same as throughout recorded history."[64]

Herr acknowledged that developments in airpower and mechanization had affected, to a great degree, the methods of cavalry employment on the modern battlefield. However, he emphasized that aircraft and mechanized vehicles were still inferior to horse cavalry in close-in reconnaissance, especially in heavily wooded areas. Likewise, he believed that only horse cavalry performed this reconnaissance in a relatively silent manner. Despite the performance of mechanized forces in the First Army maneuvers and in Poland, Herr continued to regard these formations as being useful only in areas with extensive road networks.[65]

Surprisingly, Herr began to use the situation in Europe as a positive, rather than negative, in regards to the use of horse cavalry in modern warfare. In order to demonstrate the effectiveness of horse cavalry in recent European conflicts, he argued that both the Spanish Civil War and the Polish Campaign in World War II supported the viability of horse cavalry in modern warfare. While the experiences

Cavalry detachment at the Army Day Parade in Washington, D.C. (*NARA*)

of horse cavalry during the Spanish Civil War may have supported the notion that horses had a future in modern warfare, the outbreak of World War II had altered the situation significantly. The Germans not only had large numbers of tanks but also had doctrine concerning how to employ them most effectively. Despite the fact that the Polish Campaign was both more recent and involved larger and more modern armies than the Spanish Civil War, Herr devoted an entire page in his written comments to Congress to discuss the experiences in Spain while he spent only one paragraph on Poland. He concluded his comments by stating that mechanized cavalry was "in no wise [*sic.*] suited to replace horse cavalry."[66]

As recounted earlier, the Louisiana Maneuvers of May 1940 marked the turning point for mechanization and the cavalry branch. The performance of the 7th Cavalry Brigade in battle against the 1st Cavalry Division proved conclusively that mechanized cavalry was superior to horse cavalry. On the final day of the maneuvers, Andrews organized an informal conference involving Chaffee, Brigadier General Bruce Magruder (the most senior infantry tanker), and several other of the Army's leaders on the issue of mechanization. Herr was offended that neither he nor Chief of Infantry Lynch were invited to attend the conference, though both were present during the maneuvers. Herr later stated: "The conspiracy was heading up apparently, but I am not yet clear what part Marshall may have had in this."[67] Herr believed that the conference was most likely the idea of Andrews, but "it could be that the fine Italian hand of Marshall directed it."[68]

Andrews wrote to both Herr and Lynch, asking the branch chiefs to give their views on a change in the Army's policy regarding mechanization. Lynch replied that the German Panzer units were, in effect, mechanized cavalry. He believed that it was incorrect to shape an organization on the basis of new weaponry, but rather that weapons should be adapted to missions.[69] Herr generally echoed the Chief of Infantry's reply. He believed that the then-current policy was sound and that it was a lack of funds, rather than the need for a new branch, that had delayed the development of mechanized forces. Herr also repeated Lynch's comment regarding the German forces.

> Examination of the employment of German Armored Divisions both in Poland and France show clearly that they were used on Cavalry missions.... There is no valid reason for setting up a separate corps for the development and training of units to be used in the execution of cavalry missions.[70]

He then repeated his request that the 7th Cavalry Brigade be expanded to a division, though he again made the comment that additional mechanized cavalry formations should be "provided in proportion to successive increases in the army."[71] Therefore, even at this late date, he still did not wish to dismount any other horse cavalry regiments in order to permit their mechanization.

On June 10, 1940, a more formal conference, held in Washington, D.C., determined the fate of mechanization in the Army, but this time both Herr and Lynch were invited. Andrews informed the conference participants that the only issue that was not up for debate was that two mechanized divisions were to be formed, one at Fort Knox with the 7th Cavalry Brigade as its nucleus and the other at Fort Benning with the Infantry's Provisional Tank Brigade as its nucleus. Both Herr and Lynch opposed the formation of a new branch because each believed that the cavalry and infantry were developing different kinds of mechanized vehicles for vastly different missions. Though the conference ended without any conclusive decision, Herr believed that Marshall, who he thought was rather conspicuously absent from the conference, had already made up his mind in favor of creating a new branch.[72] On June 24, 1940, the Armored Force was created.[73]

There was good reason to believe that Marshall may indeed have already made up his mind regarding this issue. First, the real experts on mechanization (Chaffee and Magruder) supported the formation of a new branch, because they had received so much resistance from the existing branches. Second, Herr had continually placed conditions on his requests for mechanized cavalry expansion. Lastly, Marshall's absence at the conference was truly conspicuous given that the meeting was called to deal with a major policy decision in the Army.

In November 1940, four months after the decision to create the separate Armored Force, Andrews forwarded a memorandum entitled "Organization

Colonel Jonathan M. Wainwright, commander of the 3rd Cavalry Regiment, *c.* 1937. (*USCM*)

U.S. Army Signal Corps cameraman filming a "charge" of the 7th Cavalry Regiment, *c.* 1930s. (*USCM*)

of the Armored Force" to the branch chiefs for their approval. The seven-page memorandum detailed the organization of the new Armored Force in not only its combat elements but also in its support units and command structure.[74] In response to this memorandum, Herr prepared a nine-page reply, which he returned to Andrews only a few weeks later. He began by refusing to concur with the recommendations presented in the original memorandum. Instead of replying to the specific details presented in the original memorandum, Herr used the first seven pages of his nine-page reply to defend his past decisions regarding mechanization. Finally, on the eighth page of his reply, Herr actually addressed the issues being discussed in the memorandum. His first criticism was that the only accomplishments of the Armored Force during the preceding four months had been the establishment of a headquarters, a school, a board, and a replacement center, all of which were activities that Herr believed could be performed by anyone who possessed sufficient funding. He then raised a legitimate point regarding the Armored Force. The tanks of the Armored Force were heavier and slower than their German counterparts and, therefore, less likely to be able to perform the traditional cavalry missions performed by similar German units.[75] Unfortunately, this legitimate point was buried so deeply in a document that otherwise sought only to defend Herr's own actions that it is doubtful if anyone in a position of authority paid any attention. Within the Army, Herr had long since become the "boy who cried wolf" and by doing so had destined the cavalry to a minor role in World War II.

In a March 13, 1941, dated personal letter to Brigadier General Innis P. Swift, commander of the 1st Cavalry Division, Herr again argued that American tanks were too heavy and slow to perform cavalry missions properly. In addition, he believed that "there will be no trouble in stopping all armored units of any character provided that intelligent methods are used."[76] Along this line of reasoning, Herr discussed the possibility of organizing new mechanized cavalry formations that relied heavily on armored cars and other light but highly mobile vehicles. This force would be mechanized and yet mobile enough to perform traditional cavalry missions. Herr believed that it was only a matter of a few months before the "cumbersome" armored divisions proved unable to perform their missions, and he wished to be able to step forward at that moment with a solution to the Army's problem. In this way, he hoped to save the cavalry branch, even if it meant the loss of the horse. Unfortunately for the cavalry branch, Herr had already waited too long.

The General Headquarters Maneuvers of 1941 was the largest and most extensive U.S. Army maneuvers ever conducted to that point. During September and November 1941, mock battles were fought in Louisiana and the Carolinas to test the Army's equipment and organization. For the cavalry, the maneuvers were a do or die situation. If the horse cavalry failed to perform well, there was little doubt that the entire cavalry would be swiftly dismounted. During the September Phase of the maneuvers in Louisiana, the 1st and 2nd Cavalry Divisions and the 56th Cavalry Brigade (Texas National Guard) performed beyond expectations, while the horse-mechanized regiments, which served as corps reconnaissance units, also performed well. The performance of the horse-mechanized regiments was particularly gratifying to Herr because he believed that it proved that his ideas regarding mechanization had been correct. Nevertheless, Captain Bruce Palmer, Jr., whose father, Colonel Bruce Palmer, had previously commanded the 1st Cavalry Regiment (Mechanized), commanded a troop of the 6th Cavalry Regiment during the maneuvers and was less exuberant about the performance of the horse-mechanized regiments. He noted that, in practice, the horse squadron tended to be ignored, while the mechanized squadron became the legitimate striking power of the regiment.[77]

During the November Phase of the maneuvers in the Carolinas, the 1st and 2nd Cavalry Divisions did not participate. Herr saw this as an attack on the horse cavalry, especially in light of their excellent performance during the first phase of the maneuvers. In addition, he believed that "artificial restrictions were imposed which would have been an absurdity in real warfare."[78] Also during the second phase of the maneuvers, the 6th and 107th (Ohio National Guard) Cavalry Regiments, which were both horse-mechanized regiments, exchanged squadrons so that 6th Cavalry had two mechanized squadrons and the 107th Cavalry had two horse squadrons. Not surprisingly, the 6th Cavalry performed far better during this phase of the maneuvers than the 107th Cavalry did.[79] Both regiments were effectively half Regular Army and half National Guard, yet the mechanized regiment had outperformed the horse regiment. This effectively negated Herr's complaint about the poor training and leadership in National Guard regiments, which he made following the First Army maneuvers at Plattsburg, New York, in 1939. Nevertheless, Herr complained that the "maneuvers were rigged to limit activities of the cavalry, for the pressure was on from certain quarters to eliminate the mounted service."[80] In a formal written evaluation of all of the forces that participated in the maneuvers, Lieutenant General Lesley J. McNair, the director of the GHQ Maneuvers, noted that while horse cavalry had performed "magnificent" physical feats during the Louisiana phase, none of their actions had equaled the accomplishments of the mechanized cavalry or armored forces.[81] The performance of the 1st and 2nd Cavalry Divisions, as well as the 56th Cavalry Brigade, certainly justified a continued investigation of horse cavalry formations. However, the superior performance of mechanized cavalry and armored formations rendered any continued investigation of horse cavalry superfluous.

Four days before the Japanese attack on Pearl Harbor, Herr delivered an address before the annual meeting of the Horse and Mule Association of America. In the address, reprinted in the *Cavalry Journal* under the title "Why Should the United States Lag Behind Other Great Powers in the Military Use of Animals?," Herr focused on the state of horse and mule use in the German and American armies. The Germans were using almost one million horses and mules for cavalry, draft, and pack purposes in their cavalry and infantry divisions, while the United States used only 38,000 horses and mules for similar purposes in their cavalry divisions—infantry divisions in the Army had completely abandoned horses and

Troopers of the 4th Cavalry Regiment (Horse-Mechanized) unloading their horses after a convoy movement, 1941. (*USCM*)

Cavalrymen eating in the field, Black Mountain Canyon, Glen Springs, Texas, 1916. (*USCM*)

mules in favor of motorized vehicles by that point.[82] These figures are somewhat misleading, however, due to the number of divisions each army possessed at the time. The German Army was composed of sixty armored and motorized divisions, as well as one cavalry and 245 infantry divisions. The U.S. Army, on the other hand, had only five armored divisions, together with two cavalry and thirty infantry divisions.[83]

In his address, Herr argued that the United States was overextending its industrial base by refusing to use horses and mules for the purpose of supply in infantry divisions. Herr believed that American industrial potential could not sustain production levels suitable to equip the United States and the majority of her allies, who were unable to produce sufficient amounts of equipment and material for their own use. Herr's rationale on this point is not completely illogical. As World War I approached its fifth year in 1919, there were drastic shortages among the Allied forces and even the addition of American industrial might seemed incapable of producing sufficient war materials. The end of the war alleviated the problem, but it was well known within the Army how close the situation had come to a major crisis. Therefore, before the American entry into World War II, it was logical for Army officers, especially veterans of World War I, to be skeptical of American industrial capabilities. Herr argued that the United States should adopt a policy for the use of animals similar to that of the German Army. The Germans used fleets of trucks only for the long haul of supplies from staging areas to infantry division headquarters. Animal transport was used to bring the supplies to the infantry itself, as the infantry could not march faster than horse-drawn vehicles.[84]

Herr also argued that the German Army, which used horse cavalry regiments as corps reconnaissance, cavalry troops as division reconnaissance, and cavalry platoons as regimental reconnaissance, spread its cavalry formations too thin and thereby had doomed itself to defeat. Larger cavalry formations could, according to Herr, act as the perfect flank support to the armored and mechanized divisions of the German Army. Herr believed that, due to weather conditions and the lack of proper roads in the Soviet Union, horse cavalry could have easily kept pace with mechanized divisions and, in many cases, outpaced them.[85]

The attack on Pearl Harbor and American entry into World War II presented Herr with the opportunity for renewed requests for horse cavalry expansion. In a memorandum to Marshall, Herr made one last attempt to save horse cavalry by urging the formation of two additional horse cavalry divisions. In order to defend his request, he pointed out the successful use of horse cavalry by the Soviet Union and the accomplishments of the 26th Cavalry Regiment (Philippine Scouts) during the ongoing Philippine Campaign. He attacked McNair, by then the commander of Army Ground Forces, as being "hostile" to horse cavalry and appealed to Marshall to overrule any objections that McNair might have.[86] Unfortunately, Herr's relationship with Marshall was too badly frayed by this point, and the open attack on another general officer (McNair) could not have helped the cause of horse cavalry in Marshall's eyes.

Air Corps officers out for a ride at Fort Riley, Kansas, *c.* 1930s. (*USCM*)

The Congressional decision to amend the National Defense Act of 1920 led to the elimination of all of the combat arms branch chiefs within the Army. Herr then found himself unassigned and he was forced to retire. Following Herr's retirement, the dismounting of the horse cavalry proceeded at a quicker pace. The decision to dismount the cavalry completely was considered by Herr to be both "unfair and, as later events seemed to prove in the rough terrains of North Africa, Sicily, [and] Italy," and "extremely unwise."[87] This is an odd statement in that each of these campaigns was an Allied victory, but he did not describe the nature of these "events." He devoted his retirement to a letter-writing campaign, which he believed would restore the horse to its previous role in the Army. The recipients of his letters were by and large cavalry officers and important individuals in the civilian government. The Secretary of War, Henry L. Stimson, was one such recipient of Herr's correspondence. Stimson, who had previously served as Secretary of War in the Taft and Franklin Roosevelt Administrations, Secretary of State in the Hoover Administration, and as a field artillery colonel during World War I, began his reply to Herr by reminding him of his allegiance to and affection for horse cavalry. Though Stimson believed that some horse cavalry should be retained "against what seems just now the very slender chance of its being useful in this war," he did not believe that there would be any need for it.[88] "But our present needs are so strongly in other directions that it seems to me that the chance of needing much Cavalry in this war is very remote."[89] Stimson ended his letter by admonishing Herr not to become bitter. "Nearly all of us have to see some of the things we love remorselessly replaced in the modern mechanized world—a world which is just as repellant to me as I think it is to you."[90]

General Lucian K. Truscott, Jr., commander (in succession) of the 3rd Infantry Division, VI Corps, and Fifth Army during World War II, was another of Herr's correspondents. Truscott agreed with Herr that not all horse cavalry should be

Secretary of State Henry Stimson inspected cavalry troops at Fort Myer, Virginia, in June 1930. (*LOC*)

eliminated and he desired to "keep alive the flame of faith."[91] He also pointed out that horses and mules saw limited use during the Italian Campaign on mounted patrols or as transport. Truscott believed, however, that it would be difficult to transport and supply large forces of cavalry overseas as a result of greater shipping priorities.[92] Colonel (later General) Hamilton H. Howze was another officer who corresponded with Herr on this issue. Howze, a horse cavalryman, had transferred to the Armored Force in 1940. He was both the nephew of Brigadier General Hamilton S. Hawkins and the son-in-law of Major General Guy V. Henry, Jr., a former Chief of Cavalry. Howze believed that "horse cavalry in the Army is through," with the exception of one or two special units.[93] More importantly, he pointed out that it was relatively unimportant whether horse cavalry should be abandoned, because "the fact is that it has been, and in my opinion will not return."[94]

Major General Ernest N. Harmon, then the commanding general of the U.S. Constabulary in occupied Germany, was also asked his opinion on the issue of horse cavalry. Harmon began by stating that Herr would not appreciate his comments, but that he would answer frankly. Horse cavalry could only fill a minor role in modern warfare, Harmon believed, specifically in mountainous country, and therefore, it would be a waste of transportation space to ship horses rather than tanks or other major implements of war.

> The horse simply cannot stand up against the carnage of modern warfare. The Germans used horse artillery in Italy to a great extent and I have seen literally hundreds, if not thousands, of dead horses over the landscape because of the effective

Captain Lucian K. Truscott, Jr., *c.* 1929. (*LOC*)

Trooper from the 13th Cavalry Regiment in Mexico, 1916. (*USCM*)

> fire of our artillery. Mechanized troops, on the other hand, traveled down roads under very heavy artillery fire without stopping and with very few casualties.[95]

Harmon went on to discuss his service in World War I and stated that he "had the definite feeling when the war [World War I] was over that the horse cavalry was obsolete from the standpoint of playing a major role in another war."[96]

In addition to his correspondence campaign, Herr also wrote a book, *Story of the U.S. Cavalry, 1775–1942*, in which he detailed the history and demise of American horse cavalry. He was convinced to the end that it had been a vast conspiracy that had caused the demise of horse cavalry:

> That there was influence brought to bear by certain industries which would profit heavily by the production of the enormously expensive tank and other mechanized vehicles is almost certain. Then, there was the ever-eternal green-eyed monster of jealousy which had been aroused in the breasts of the other services, especially among soft and inactive officers behind desks, over the color and glamour attached to the cavalry, over the good times which the officers of that branch enjoyed in their sports at all the cavalry posts, and over the certain indefinable social prestige which the man on horse, the cavalier, the *hidalgo*, the gentleman, has always had over

Trooper and his mount both wearing gas masks, Fort Riley, Kansas, *c.* 1939. (*USCM*)

> the man on foot. All these influences combined, and, amidst the excitement at the outbreak of war, managed to eliminate what they called an archaic branch.[97]

As with Hawkins, Herr ultimately admitted that his advocacy of the horse was a matter of faith and not of empirical evidence.

As demonstrated, the supporters of the horse were opposed to mechanization and ultimately revealed that their attitudes were based primarily on traditionalism. Despite the obvious and significant contributions mechanized forces made in the opening phases of World War II in Europe and the two massive Army maneuvers in Louisiana and the Carolinas, Hawkins and Herr refused to admit that horses had become obsolete. Further, even after American involvement in World War II began, these men refused to revise their earlier statements. In fact, Herr continued to agitate for horse cavalry even after the Korean War.[98] Hawkins and Herr represent the most traditional and short-sighted elements within the cavalry. Unfortunately, these two men, rather than the "modernizers," continue to be the defining image of horse cavalrymen for the majority of Americans.

4

"Modernizers": Proponents of Mechanization

During the period following the enactment of the National Defense Act of 1920, most cavalry officers realized that supporting mechanization was detrimental to their futures in the U.S. Army. The War Department decided that tanks were the exclusive purview of the infantry, and all officers were expected to obey, regardless of their personal opinions. While, on the whole, most officers complied, a few devoted individuals believed that the future of cavalry lay not with the horse but with mechanized vehicles. The most prominent of these supporters of mechanization, who could accurately be termed "modernizers," were Lieutenant General Daniel Van Voorhis, Major General Adna R. Chaffee, Jr., Major General Guy V. Henry, Jr., and Major General Leon B. Kromer.

As with the all cavalry officers of the period, the careers of 'modernizers', such as Adna R. Chaffee, Jr., developed through traditional horse cavalry activities. Chaffee was born into an Army family at Fort Riley, Kansas, in 1884. His father, Lieutenant General Adna R. Chaffee, Sr., served as the U.S. Army Chief of Staff between 1904 and 1906, and Chaffee Jr. graduated from the United States Military Academy (USMA) at West Point, New York, in 1906. Most of his time before World War I was filled with polo matches and horse shows. Chaffee was one of the best polo players and horsemen in the Army. He was even sent to France to continue his education in horsemanship, where he attended *l'École d'application de Cavalerie* at Saumur, France.[1]

Only after his appointment as an Assistant Instructor in the Department of Tactics at West Point in 1915, Chaffee, by then a captain, began for the first time to seriously study the art of warfare.[2] Following the United States declaration of war against Germany in April 1917, Chaffee was transferred to Camp Jackson, South Carolina, where he served as the acting Chief of Staff of the 81st Division for three months. Arriving in France in February 1918, he attended the American Expeditionary Force Staff College at Langres, which proved to be another pivotal assignment in his career. Chaffee did so well at the Staff College that, despite his desire for a combat assignment, he was made a member of the faculty. It was

Second Lieutenant Adna R. Chaffee, Jr., *c.* 1908. (*LOC*)

his service as a staff officer that brought him many of his greatest opportunities throughout the rest of his career. During October 1918, Chaffee served as the Assistant Chief of Staff for Operations (G-3) and the acting Chief of Staff of the VII Corps followed by service as the G-3 for the III Corps from November 1918 until July 1919.[3]

During the three short years between his posting to West Point and the end of World War I, Chaffee transformed himself from a dilettante polo player into a serious and highly respected staff officer. He also now reevaluated the horse cavalryman lifestyle that he had once so fondly embraced. In 1925, Major General Malin Craig, the Chief of Cavalry, offered Chaffee the opportunity to serve as the head of the Department of Horsemanship at the Cavalry School, Fort Riley, Kansas. Chaffee rejected the offer because his experience in World War I convinced him that the horse was no longer as important in modern warfare.[4] In rejecting Craig's offer, Chaffee privileged his convictions over his career advancement, as, had he accepted, he presumably would have resumed a career path that may even have taken him in his father's footsteps—possibly to U.S. Army Chief of Staff. His refusal to accept this offer alienated him from the cavalry branch, which meant that he had to rely on staff appointments for career advancement.[5] In fact, the 1920s were a decade during which Chaffee moved from staff to teaching to student assignments with only a single command.[6]

U.S. Army Chief of Staff General Malin Craig in October 1935. (*LOC*)

In December 1928, Chaffee was serving in the G-3 Section of the War Department General Staff. Though he had no experience with tanks, Chaffee was impressed by the Experimental Mechanized Force maneuvers at Camp Meade. As a member of the War Department Mechanization Board, he prepared the first official proposal for the creation of a permanent and independent mechanized force.[7] Chaffee's proposal was not acted upon immediately due to budgetary concerns, but it served as a blueprint for the eventual formation of the 1st Cavalry Regiment (Mechanized).

Following his decision regarding horse cavalry, Chaffee's career choices thereafter reflected this conviction. In a lecture delivered at the Army War College in 1929, he publicly identified himself with mechanization by discussing the current and desired future trends in mechanized combat. He stated that each nation identified its own needs in respect to mechanization. In the United Kingdom, for instance, the British were seriously entertaining the thought that it would be preferable for a future British Expeditionary Force to possess three mechanized divisions, rather than the previous deployment of six traditional infantry divisions. In France, in contrast, since the army anticipated engaging primarily in defensive operations, tanks and other mechanized vehicles were seen as nothing more than an adjunct of the infantry.[8] Chaffee's assertions regarding the British and French proved to be close to the mark. In 1940, the British Expeditionary Force, while it did contain traditional infantry divisions, used only motorized vehicles. The officers of the French Army, with the notable exception of Charles de Gaulle, continued to view the tank as a mere auxiliary weapon in their defensive strategy. Though British and French armies viewed the tank primarily as an infantry support vehicle, their combined forces possessed more tanks, including many fast "cavalry" tanks, than the Germans in 1940.

Chaffee also outlined the limitations that he believed existed in regards to mechanized vehicles in the U.S. Army. Firstly, he did not believe that the Army could be completely mechanized, because the United States did not have the industrial capacity to do so. Secondly, he believed that mechanized vehicles suffered from severe limitations, namely, that they were not impervious to artillery, were too noisy for night operations or surprise attacks, could be stopped by more natural and man-made obstacles than infantry, and were of little value in defensive operations because they could not "dig in."[9] At the time, Chaffee's assertions were correct. The Great Depression had contracted the American economy and, in addition, Chaffee, as a veteran of World War I, was well aware of the supply problems that American forces faced in 1918. In addition, mechanized vehicles of the time did indeed suffer from many severe limitations. The question remained as to whether these limitations could be overcome. It appears that while Chaffee recognized that the limitations, he also believed that they could be overcome in time—otherwise it is unlikely that he would have risked his professional career by defending mechanization.

Mess Hall at the encampment near Glen Springs, Texas, 1916. Sixty-seven days after the attack on Columbus, New Mexico, troops under Francisco "Pancho" Villa attacked this encampment and killed three soldiers. (*USCM*)

Chaffee believed that mechanized units would be best organized as division-sized formations, which corps commanders could use to achieve local breakthroughs. The mechanized divisions acted as the tip of the spear, which opened a hole in the enemy defenses—allowing the slower infantry divisions to exploit that opening. In Chaffee's vision, the mechanized divisions would be combined arms formations containing cavalry, infantry, artillery, engineer, and other supporting arms. The units from each of the traditional branches, however, would be mechanized in order for them to keep up with the main force of tanks.[10] The organization of the Army during World War II reflected Chaffee's vision.

As a result of his identification as a pro-mechanization officer, Chaffee, after his promotion to lieutenant colonel, reported to Fort Eustis, Virginia, to become the executive officer of the Mechanized Force. At this stage, with the future of mechanization far from certain, Chaffee was offered a way out. Brigadier General Walter C. Short, then the commander of the 1st Cavalry Division at Fort Bliss, Texas, offered Chaffee the position of division Chief of Staff, an opportunity that Short believed would save Chaffee's professional career.[11] While Chaffee was enthusiastic about the offer, he decided against accepting it:

> I think it is probably one of the best positions that an officer of my rank in the Army could occupy, and one of the best opportunities he could have. However, I have been associated with mobile mechanization in the Army since its inception, [and] … I feel I should stay with it until the War Department makes a decision in the matter.[12]

Chaffee's decision was ultimately fortuitous, but at the time, it demonstrated his commitment to the concept of mechanization.

The commitment that Chaffee felt for mechanization was not only seen when he served with mechanized units. Chaffee eventually transferred back to the War Department General Staff as a member of the Budget and Legislative Planning Board. In this position, he was able to appropriate funds for the mechanized cavalry that most likely would not have been forthcoming otherwise. In 1939, Chaffee's effectiveness in this role was pointed out indirectly by Lieutenant Colonel James Weaver, a battalion commander in the 66th Infantry Regiment (Light Tanks):

> I saw the cavalry get everything it asked for including the non-statute [*sic.*] light tank [M-2] by calling it a combat car; I saw them get 56 so-called combat cars when all we got was 18; I saw them get $600,000 of the President's reserve for equipment of the cavalry mechanized brigade.[13]

Thus Chaffee's transfer allowed him to continue to support mechanization in a different way.

Chaffee frequently lectured on the subject of mechanized cavalry to the Army War College. During a September 1939 lecture, he provided a long and detailed history of mechanized cavalry in the U.S. Army and discussed the future in light

“Combat Car” from Troop C, 1st Cavalry Regiment (Mechanized), Fort Knox, Kentucky, *c*. 1937. (*USCM*)

of the German invasion of Poland. Chaffee included in his lecture many of the same points he had previously made in other lectures and memoranda.[14] Major Robert W. Grow, a member of the mechanized cavalry clique then serving in the Office of the Chief of Cavalry, attended Chaffee’s lecture and afterward wrote that it was the best discussion on mechanized cavalry that he had ever heard. Over cocktails after the lecture, Chaffee told Grow that “he was going to have a division and [was] going to get the necessary men even if they have to come from horse units.”[15] Chaffee also “bet me $5 that I would not be in the Philippines, where I was scheduled to be, on 1 August 1940. How well he foresaw the future. I was actually the G-3 of the 2nd Armored Division on 1 August 1940.”[16] Though he served as the first chief of the independent Armored Force after its creation in 1940, Chaffee did not live to see the great accomplishments of American tankers in World War II. He died of cancer on 22 August 1941.

Another of the cavalry “modernizers” of the interwar period was Daniel Van Voorhis. In October 1930, on the orders of the U.S. Army Chief of Staff, General Charles P. Summerall, the previously short-lived Mechanized Force was permanently reestablished and Van Voorhis, a colonel then commanding the 12th Cavalry Regiment, was chosen as the first commander of the “permanent” Mechanized Force. Though Van Voorhis was not identified with the pro-mechanization faction in the cavalry, he and his staff eventually became a devoted supporters of cavalry mechanization. Among his staff were Major Sereno E. Brett, a former World War I tanker and later a brigadier general, and Major Robert W. Grow, who would become a major general and command the 3rd and 6th Armored Divisions during World War II.

Van Voorhis was born in Zanesville, Ohio, on October 24, 1878, and began his military career as a corporal in the 10th Pennsylvania Volunteer Infantry Regiment during the Spanish-American War. After rising to the rank of captain during the war, he was offered the opportunity to be commissioned in the newly expanded Regular Army.[17] After accepting that commission in 1900, Van Voorhis had a varied career before America's entry in World War I.[18] During World War I, Van Voorhis served as a staff officer and embarkation/debarkation port commander in the United States and later in France. In the 1920s, he served in command positions, in the Office of the Chief of Cavalry, and as a student at the Army War College.[19]

The "permanent" Mechanized Force was later re-designated the 1st Cavalry Regiment (Mechanized). After the re-designation, Van Voorhis envisioned the

Officers attending the Advanced Equitation Class at the Cavalry School, Fort Riley, Kansas, 1938. (*USCM*)

necessity for more than a single mechanized cavalry regiment. In a memorandum to the U.S. Army G-3 dated May 5, 1931, a mere four days after the Chief of Staff, General Douglas MacArthur, decided to re-designate the Mechanized Force, Van Voorhis proposed the creation of an entire mechanized cavalry brigade. In the same memorandum, he also suggested that Camp Meade, Maryland, then home of the Mechanized Force, was unsuitable for the proper evaluation of mechanized techniques. Interestingly, Van Voorhis opposed the idea of moving the re-designated Force to Fort Riley, Kansas, where the cavalry branch's school was located. He publically objected because he believed that the presence of mechanized cavalry at the same post as the home of horse cavalry might have an adverse effect on the school, but with the implied idea that the opposite might also be true.[20] After more staff duty from 1934 to 1937, Van Voorhis was promoted to brigadier general and commanded the 7th Cavalry Brigade (Mechanized).

In a 1937 letter to the Chief of Cavalry, Major General Leon B. Kromer, Van Voorhis demonstrated his innovative but practical approach to mechanization by outlining the possible organization of a mechanized cavalry division. First, Van Voorhis stated that the innovations already developed by the cavalry proved themselves both sound and valuable, since infantry tankers used the cavalry's combat car, scout car, and .50-caliber machine gun.[21] Second, the

Second Lieutenant J. H. Polk, Fort Riley, Kansas, 1938. (*USCM*)

Second Army Maneuvers of 1936 convinced Van Voorhis that 500 was the maximum number of tanks that could be properly employed in a division-sized formation.[22] With that in mind, he believed that a mechanized cavalry division needed no more than two mechanized regiments as its combat element. Third, the division required at least four batteries of field artillery, with two of the four being self-propelled and the remaining two batteries towed by trucks.[23] Fourth, the division needed a reconnaissance and support squadron made up of an armored car troop for reconnaissance and a troop of riflemen mounted in a fast moving, though lightly armored, chassis for support.[24] During World War II, the Army used vehicles similar to the type Van Voorhis described—the M2/M3/M5 Half-tracks. Lastly, the division required a signal company, an engineering company, a medical company, an ordnance company, and a quartermaster company, all motorized or mechanized.[25] Van Voorhis argued that the first of these mechanized cavalry divisions should be organized at Fort Knox with the 7th Cavalry Brigade as its basis. Later divisions would then be organized at Fort Riley and Fort Bliss, Texas. Van Voorhis' mechanized cavalry division was organizationally quite similar to the U.S. Army armored divisions that fought in World War II.

Even after giving up the command of the 7th Cavalry Brigade, Van Voorhis continued to support mechanization in his other assignments. He was eventually promoted to major general and given command of the V Corps, headquartered at Fort Hayes, Ohio, which meant that Fort Knox, then the home of mechanized cavalry, was within his command area.[26] Van Voorhis' example demonstrated that support for mechanization was not limited to younger officers, influenced by their experiences during World War I. Van Voorhis had served in the nineteenth-century Spanish-American War, but became one of the first and most significant supporters of mechanization during the twentieth century. He even continued his support even when his career took him to assignments away from Fort Knox and the 7th Cavalry Brigade.

During the 1930s, two Chiefs of Cavalry in succession, Major Generals Guy V. Henry, Jr., and Leon B. Kromer, also played significant roles in the process of mechanization. Henry, a close friend of Chaffee during his polo-playing days and the son and grandson of West Point graduates, was born at Fort Robinson, Nebraska, on January 28, 1875. After graduating from West Point in 1898, he held the rank of major in the 26th U.S. Volunteer Infantry Regiment during the Spanish-American War. Following eighteen years of traditional cavalry service, Henry, by then a colonel, was the commandant of cadets at West Point between 1916 and 1918.[27] Promoted to brigadier general, he simultaneously took command of the 15th Division, its component 29th Infantry Brigade, and Camp Logan, Texas, on September 11, 1918.[28] As the 15th Division was demobilized in January 1919, Henry transferred to Camp Beauregard, Louisiana, as the new camp commander from January 30 to March 31, 1919.[29] During the 1920s, Henry followed the traditional career path of an officer marked for important responsibilities.[30]

Major Guy V. Henry in 1919. (*LOC*)

In 1930, Henry became the Chief of Cavalry and soon after a great ally of mechanization. His support of mechanization was exhibited in an article he wrote for the *Cavalry Journal* in 1932 regarding the future trends toward the organization and equipment of cavalry forces throughout the world. In the article, the majority of his references to the Cavalry discussed the positive opportunities offered by mechanization:

> Our cavalry officers are sincerely interested in mechanization. With proper financial and official support they may be relied upon to develop mechanized and horse cavalries suitable to our needs ... both manned by men of the same tactical training, quickness of thought, courage, *élan*, and determination to close with the enemy that for centuries has been the spirit of cavalry.[31]

Henry also noted that, although an American horse cavalry division mustered a greater rate of small arms firepower per man than its European counterparts, the American division possessed only one armored car squadron and one tank company. Likewise, the division lacked sufficient trucks to move its supplies and possessed almost no anti-tank or anti-aircraft defenses. In Henry's opinion, therefore, an American cavalry division was under-motorized, under-mechanized, and under-armored.[32] Henry also discussed the mechanized cavalry regiment which was then being developed and which he believed was perfectly suited to the cavalry, since it relied heavily on the most important attributes of the Cavalry—mobility and firepower. These comments, which were a matter of public record, clearly identified Henry, the Chief of Cavalry, with the pro-mechanization faction in the cavalry branch. Henry believed that the majority of cavalry officers were indeed interested in mechanization. It was only the lack of proper financial and official support that prevented the expansion of mechanized cavalry.

Henry's support for mechanization was not only limited to public speeches, he privately defended mechanization against its detractors. In December 1932, Brigadier General Abraham G. Lott, the Commandant of the Cavalry School, forwarded a letter to Henry from Colonel Selwyn D. Smith, commander of the 2nd Cavalry Regiment at Fort Riley. In the letter, Smith stated that an improved horse cavalry organization would be able to "combat mechanization and prevent the latter from assuming the principal cavalry strategical [*sic.*] functions."[33] Henry replied to Lott with a letter that strongly reminded him what role the Cavalry School exercised in the Army:

> Attention is invited to this quotation because it conveys the thought that the Cavalry School is seeking to prevent the development of mechanization. This belief was held by certain individuals in the War Department and was a strong contributory reason why Mechanized Cavalry was not sent to Fort Riley for station. The role of the Cavalry School is to develop our own cavalry, horsed and mechanized, to their highest point of efficiency.[34]

Above: Major General Guy V. Henry (left), Chief of Cavalry, presenting the Goodrich Trophy, awarded annually to the U.S. Cavalry troop showing the best all-around performance, to Captain A. M. Shelton, commander of Troop E, 3rd Cavalry Regiment at Fort Myer, Virginia. (*LOC*)

Left: Major General Guy V. Henry being sworn in the Chief of Cavalry at Fort Meyer, Virginia.
Left to right: Henry and Major S. V. Constant, Post Adjutant. (*LOC*)

Lott's reply was to explain that Henry had misunderstood the intent of Smith's letter. According to Lott, Smith meant that improved horse cavalry organization could defeat a mechanized enemy. Lott went on to assure Henry that both he and Smith were committed to producing the most effective cavalry force possible, whether horse or mechanized or some combination thereof.[35]

In order to continue his support for mechanization after completing his four-year tenure as Chief of Cavalry, Henry accepted a voluntary reduction in rank and, as a brigadier general, became commander of the 7th Cavalry Brigade (Mechanized). After commanding the 7th Cavalry Brigade for a year, Henry was offered the position of Commandant of the Cavalry School. Though he continued to support mechanization, he felt compelled to accept the appointment, because he believed that he could do more good for the cavalry as a whole at Fort Riley.[36]

The second Chief of Cavalry, who played a significant role in the process of mechanization, was Leon B. Kromer. Born in Grand Rapids, Michigan, on June 25, 1876, and graduated from West Point in 1899, Kromer saw combat in the Philippine Insurrection, participated in the Mexican Punitive Expedition, and served two tours as an instructor at West Point. During World War I, Kromer was the Assistant Chief of Staff for Logistics (S-4) of the 82nd Division and briefly the acting Assistant Chief of Staff for Operations (G-3) for the I Corps.[37] Finally, he served as the Assistant Chief of Staff for Personnel (G-1) for the First Army from October 1918 until April 1919.[38] Prior to his appointment as Chief of Cavalry, Kromer spent most of the 1920s and early 1930s on staff duty.[39]

Sergeant Sylvester A. Merritt, Headquarters Troop, 8th Cavalry Regiment, Fort Bliss, Texas, 1933. (*USCM*)

Following his appointment as Chief of Cavalry in 1934, Kromer supported mechanization in a variety of ways. An example of this support was a 1934 lecture Kromer delivered to the Army War College on both the status of the cavalry branch and the results of recent cavalry maneuvers at Fort Riley. His lecture pointed out that mechanized cavalry was superior to horse cavalry in traditional cavalry roles, though it was more sensitive to some natural and man-made obstacles. Kromer believed that the scout cars and armored cars of the horse cavalry regiments not only allowed them to reconnoiter larger areas but also prevented the horse cavalry from being "blind" on the modern battlefield. The vastly superior firepower of mechanized cavalry meant that horse cavalry was unable to directly engage it and was relegated to mere harassment actions. Kromer concluded his lecture by calling for the mechanization of a second cavalry regiment in order to fill out the 7th Cavalry Brigade.[40] As a result of these maneuvers and doubtless other data, Kromer believed that horse cavalry no longer played a major role on the modern battlefield. Under these conditions, mechanized cavalry performed the traditional cavalry roles, while offering greater mobility and firepower.

Another example of Kromer's support for mechanization was an organizational plan he submitted to the General Staff. The plan called for a far greater expansion of cavalry mechanization than anyone else had previously proposed, since he wanted to mechanize three more regiments in order to complete the organization of the 7th Cavalry Brigade and supply one mechanized cavalry regiment for each of the existing cavalry divisions (1st and 2nd Cavalry Divisions). In addition, he wanted to create nine armored car squadrons to serve as corps reconnaissance for each corps in the Army.[41]

Brigadier General John H. Hughes, the U.S. Army G-3, replied to Kromer's requests by asking him to justify the increases in light of the budgetary constraints under which the Army was then operating.[42] Kromer responded by saying that his requests were in line with the mandates issued to the cavalry by Chief of Staff General Douglas MacArthur in May 1931.[43] Though Kromer's larger goals were not met, his persistence did pay off when the 1st Battalion, 68th Field Artillery Regiment, was motorized and added to the 7th Cavalry Brigade.[44]

After the 7th Cavalry Brigade finally became a brigade-sized formation in 1936, Kromer continued to propose further expansion. In a memorandum, Kromer noted that the Germans were creating a Panzer Corps of three divisions, the Italians were likeminded, and the British and French had each mechanized one cavalry division. Kromer noted that the Germans had no horses whatsoever in their Panzer Corps: "The German Cavalry was offered the Panzer Corps in 1933 but turned it down, and as a result [the cavalry] has been greatly reduced."[45] Kromer clearly envisioned a potential problem for the cavalry and wished to deal with the problem before it happened. To this end, he asked Van Voorhis about the possibility of creating a mechanized cavalry division or possibly even a mechanized cavalry corps. However, there was no funding available for either expansion.

On January 22, 1938, Missouri Senator Harry Truman (right) watches the 7th Cavalry Brigade (Mechanized) pass in review. Brigadier General Daniel Van Voorhis points out something to Truman while Lieutenant Colonel Willis Crittenberger functions as the master of ceremonies. (*USCM*)

Panoramic view of the 13th Cavalry Regiment (Mechanized) at Fort Knox, Kentucky in June 1938. (*LOC*)

As Kromer entered his last year as Chief of Cavalry, he continued to fight for mechanization, though sometimes in ways that were not always obvious. In March 1937, he appointed Lieutenant Colonel Willis D. Crittenberger, then the S-3 (Operations and Training) officer of the 7th Cavalry Brigade, as an instructor at the Command and General Staff School. Crittenberger wrote to Kromer to request that he be given command of a mechanized cavalry squadron in the 1st or 13th Cavalry Regiments instead. Kromer, however, believed that Crittenberger could do more good for both the cavalry and the Army as a whole by instructing the CGSS students in mechanized cavalry than he could by commanding a mechanized cavalry squadron.[46]

In a lecture on cavalry delivered to the Army War College in October 1937, Kromer once again used the opportunity to defend the continued development of mechanized cavalry. He used the development of mechanized forces in the major European powers to support his opinions regarding mechanization in the U.S. Army. In Germany, the army no longer possessed even a single cavalry division. Though fourteen cavalry regiments did exist on paper, the Germans had divided these regiments into corps and division reconnaissance units. Of the five cavalry divisions in the French Army, two had been mechanized, while approximately one-third of the combat power of the three remaining divisions was mechanized. In the United Kingdom, no division-sized formation of cavalry existed, but Kromer quoted the American military *attaché* as stating: "The entire British Regular Army, *so far as its operations in Europe are concerned*, is to be mechanized, lock, stock and barrel."[47] Kromer then turned his attention toward the U.S. Cavalry and made a statement that would have surprised many cavalrymen:

> Cavalry welcomes any mechanized development that will increase its effectiveness. If, in the future, we develop any breed or breeds of iron horse that can prove superior to the thoroughbred for all cavalry missions, we will abandon the horse.[48]

Kromer made it clear that cavalry did not need horses if suitable mechanized vehicles could perform traditional cavalry missions.

Following the lecture, Major Robert W. Grow, who was then serving in the Office of the Chief of Cavalry, wrote about how much he approved of the directness of Kromer's comments. At that time, Grow wrote that there seemed no

Sergeant Samuel MacDonald, Troop G, 2nd Cavalry Regiment, Fort Riley, Kansas, *c.* 1929. (*USCM*)

question that the future of the cavalry as a combat arm was definitely in jeopardy. It appeared to him that Kromer also realized that this was the case and that he was willing to support mechanization even at the expense of horse cavalry. Grow believed that had Kromer (or someone of a similar mindset) remained Chief of Cavalry, then the Armored Force would never have been created and the cavalry would have remained the Army's maneuver branch.[49] Unfortunately for the Cavalry, however, Kromer's tour as Chief of Cavalry came to an end, and he was succeeded by someone who had a completely different attitude toward mechanization—namely John K. Herr.

It is interesting to note that the supporters of mechanization did not always have unanimity of opinion as to how to achieve their ends. In 1936, the decision to complete the organization of the 7th Cavalry Brigade with one of the two cavalry regiments stationed at Fort Riley, prompted Henry, who was a longtime supporter of mechanization, to opposition. He did not oppose mechanizing one of the regiments but rather its transfer to Fort Knox. In a memorandum, Henry argued that it was impossible for him to properly instruct the officers and non-commissioned officers sent to the Cavalry School without two complete cavalry regiments. He agreed that a second regiment needed to be mechanized and sent to Fort Knox. Henry also believed that it would be beneficial for the cavalry to have a mechanized regiment at Fort Riley:

> In making this recommendation I make it as a sincere friend of mechanization, believing greatly in its possibilities, and with as thorough a knowledge of it as any officer in the United States Army.... With one horse and one mechanized regiment here, the Cavalry School can carry on and carry on well.... I personally would, if conditions would permit, greatly like to see the 7th Cavalry Brigade (Mecz.) organized and concentrated at Fort Knox, but to do that at the expense of the Cavalry School would be a mistake. No matter how our cavalry is transported or fights ... the basis of its instruction must be ... along the principles now taught at the Cavalry School.[50]

Henry further argued that it would be far easier to house a mechanized regiment at Fort Riley than at Fort Knox. Since he had recently served as the post commander at Fort Knox, Henry was acutely aware of the shortage of housing there. Though Henry's objections were acknowledged, the decision was made to mechanize one of the regiments at Fort Riley, otherwise no cavalry regiment would be mechanized. With this in mind, the 13th Cavalry Regiment, commanded by Colonel Charles L. Scott, was dismounted and transferred to Fort Knox.[51]

It appears that Henry would have preferred the mechanization of two separate cavalry regiments—one for Fort Riley and the other to complete the organization of the 7th Cavalry Brigade. Since money for two additional mechanized cavalry regiments was not forthcoming, however, he had to accept the inevitable and part with one of his regiments. It is debatable as to whether a mechanized cavalry regiment at Fort Riley might have actually done more good for the process of mechanization than its placement at Fort Knox. Henry was correct that Fort

M3 tank and Armored Force trainee completing the course at Fort Benning, Georgia. (*NARA*)

Saddle Room, Fort Worth, Texas, *c.* 1935. (*USCM*)

Knox was horribly overcrowded and that Fort Riley offered a better location in a spatial sense. It might also be argued that the presence of a mechanized cavalry regiment at Fort Riley, where cavalry officers attended their basic and advanced courses, might have prompted more interest in mechanization among typical cavalry officers. Nevertheless, the counter-argument was that without a second regiment to complete its organization, the 7th Cavalry Brigade could not have formulated doctrine for units larger than regiments.

Many factors influenced the decision to create the independent Armored Force to oversee mechanization in the Army during World War II. The most decisive of these factors was the role of various "modernizer" individuals who had the seniority and authority to make mechanization a lasting reality. Van Voorhis, Henry, and Kromer were all important members of this group of "modernizer" officers. However, undoubtedly the most important of these "modernizers" was Chaffee. It was Chaffee's conception of mechanization that ultimately triumphed at the expense of both the cavalry and infantry branches. Chaffee had been associated with mechanization longer than any other cavalry officer, and by 1940, he was the only senior cavalry officer still directly involved with mechanization. He was also the first chief of the new Armored Force. His efforts rewarded not only himself but also the Army as a whole. It was the Armored Force that played such a significant role in the American victories in Europe during World War II.

5

"Pragmatists": Attitudes Among the Army's Future Leaders

During the interwar period, while some cavalry officers voiced opinions for or against mechanization, most maintained the *status quo*. It is difficult to determine why these officers did not voice opinions for or against mechanization, but most likely they either had no opinion or decided to "play it safe" by not voicing their opinions. Therefore, their attitude on this issue was completely logical and "pragmatic." Unfortunately, it is almost impossible to document their rationale since people generally did not write articles or memoirs about how they were indifferent or pragmatic. The few accounts from these officers tend to show that they trusted the Army to provide the correct equipment/weaponry in time for the next war.[1]

The complex intellectual atmosphere of the interwar U.S. Army yielded a variety of perspectives on the issue of mechanization, including the opinions of CGSS students at the U.S. Army's Command and General Staff School (CGSS) at Fort Leavenworth, Kansas. The CGSS was the main post-graduate institution for officers within the Army during the interwar period. Student thoughts and opinions on mechanization, expressed in a variety of academic papers, suggest an intellectual consensus of the emerging leadership that later shaped the Army's dominant perspective on the use of mechanized vehicles. These papers also reveal a delicate process of negotiation between "traditional" and "modernizer" views—an attempt to legitimize innovation through reference to the past. Indeed, the papers provide rare insight into a rationalization process that supported and justified the changes. The papers that survive reveal mindsets that perceived no huge opposition between tradition and mechanization. In fact, most of the arguments made by the CGSS students attempted to show not how mechanization revolutionized warfare, but rather how it strengthened and augmented traditional forms or, in the case of one paper, revived an older, traditional method considered obsolete. To the CGSS students, tradition and mechanization were not irreconcilable extremes. An examination of the surviving interwar student papers demonstrates that the CGSS students who discussed the topic of mechanization

Second Lieutenant J. H. Polk, Fort Riley, Kansas, 1938. (*USCM*)

believed that it was a positive development. The only question was how far mechanization would ultimately progress.

The Command and General Staff School was the result of educational reforms initiated by Secretary of War Elihu Root, who served under President Theodore Roosevelt at the turn of the twentieth century. Root was responsible for instituting the modern general staff system in the U.S. Army. An effective general staff required highly educated officers, and accordingly, the Army higher education system was structured to produce officers capable of high-level staff duty. In addition, since the Army was traditionally so small and underfunded, there were few chances for field maneuvers involving large numbers of troops. Thus the CGSS offered opportunities for educating/training officers for both staff duty and the operational level of warfare.[2]

During the interwar period, the curriculum of the CGSS went through four distinct phases. From 1919 to 1923, Leavenworth resumed the pre-World War I organization of a first-year course, called the School of the Line, and a second-year course, the General Staff School, to which only about 50 percent of the first-year students were admitted. The School of the Line focused on command of brigades and divisions and staff duty at the division level. The General Staff School focused on command of corps and armies as well as staff duty at those levels.[3] During the second phase from 1923 to 1929, the two schools were consolidated to create the Command and General Staff School, which offered a one-year course. The CGSS focused on command and staff duty at the division and corps level.[4] The third phase from 1929 to 1936 saw the course returned to two years in length, however, all officers who attended the first year automatically stayed for the second year. The curriculum did not change appreciably, but more time was now allowed for an in-depth study of subjects.[5] The fourth and final phase of the CGSS prior to World War II occurred between 1936 and 1940. During this last phase, the course returned to a single year and the curriculum focused primarily at command and staff duties at the division level.[6]

The CGSS students during this period were among the best and brightest in the Army—on average slightly less than 10 percent of Army majors attended CGSS annually.[7] Within the interwar Army, officers identified by senior leaders as the "best brains" spent a significant amount of their careers on staff duty, in school, or teaching. The more time an officer spent at these activities, the better a chance he had for future high command. In 1955, the Command and General Staff College (CGSC) prepared a study in which they examined class standing at CGSS/CGSC as a measure of career potential.[8] Though the study did not provide convenient statistical breakdown, it did reveal that those officers who finished higher in their classes tended to attain higher ranks during World War II. For example, Dwight D. Eisenhower—who was eventually one of only four Generals of the Army in U.S. history—graduated first (out of 245) in the Class of 1926. Omar N. Bradley, also a future General of the Army, graduated first (out of eighty-eight) in the Class of 1929.[9] An examination of the data provided in the study revealed that all eight of the four-star generals on active duty in 1955 finished in the top third of their classes and only one of the twenty-eight Lieutenant Generals on active duty in 1955 had not graduated from the CGSS/CGSC.[10]

The only surviving student papers from the interwar CGSS come from the 1929 to 1936 phase when every student attended for two years and was required to produce a research paper. Among the subjects covered by these research papers were many diverse and often experimental topics. CGSS students from all Army branches were encouraged to produce research papers about topics that lay outside their expertise or that they might not otherwise consider. Examples of this cross-pollination are a quartermaster officer who produced a research paper on armored and aviation reconnaissance, an air corps officer who produced a research paper on the use of armored vehicles with horse cavalry, and an infantry officer who produced a research paper on a cavalry training pamphlet. In this intellectually inquisitive environment, CGSS students were allowed to explore possibilities that were not necessarily given as much consideration in the Army as a whole. As a result, some research papers discussed the divisive topic of mechanization within the cavalry.

The CGSS students not only discussed the issue of mechanization but also defined the schools of thought involved in the debate. In 1932, Major John T.

Trick horse "Buster" of Troop F, 8th Cavalry Regiment, Fort Bliss, Texas, 1924. (*USCM*)

Sergeant Samuel MacDonald with troopers of the Machine Gun Troop, 2nd Cavalry Regiment, Fort Riley, Kansas, *c*. 1927. (*USCM*)

Pierce, a cavalry officer, discussed the two "Colleges" that he believed existed on the question of mechanization. The first was identified as the "Garage College," which believed "that wars of the future will be fought entirely by small mechanized armies, [and] that future battlefields will be unmarked by the footprints of man or animal."[11] The second was identified as the "Conservative College," which believed "that future wars will be fought, and won, by men, as have all past wars, but that the man on the battlefield will be assisted to the greatest extent possible by every use of modern appliances."[12]

In 1934, Captain Norman McNeill, an infantry officer, also discussed the two groups involved in the debate over mechanization. McNeill consulted both the American and British *Cavalry Journal*s as well as several other works available in the CGSS library and then divided the authors into two groups. The majority believed that mechanized cavalry remained an auxiliary to horse cavalry. Nevertheless, a smaller group of writers went to "visionary extremes." These "visionary extremes" predicted that mechanized forces would, in time, supersede horse cavalry formations in traditional cavalry roles.[13]

In 1936, Major James T. Curry, Jr., an air corps officer, admitted that most military thinkers agreed that a war of movement would characterize future warfare. However, these same thinkers had not reached a consensus as to how to achieve mobile warfare. Curry also believed that two "Colleges" of thought existed on this issue. The first "College," which he defined as "extremists," believed that the foot soldier and horse cavalry were no longer be relevant and that future armies would be smaller and completely mechanized. The other "College" believed that traditional infantry and cavalry would be supplemented, but not replaced, in the future by the addition of trucks and other mechanical vehicles.[14]

In 1933, Captain Francis T. Bonsteel, a cavalry officer, argued that there were three categories of opinion on the issue of mechanization. The first category, which he referred to as "extremists," believed that except for operations in difficult terrain, traditional infantry, cavalry, and artillery would be replaced by smaller, completely mechanized forces. The second category, basing their beliefs exclusively on the performance of mechanized vehicles during World War I, believed that mechanized formations had no place anywhere other than static or trench warfare. The third and "more moderate opinion" held that any full-scale future war would be fought by nations utilizing the most modern and effective forces possible. As a result, they would use any forces which could prove themselves in battle.[15] Bonsteel believed that most military experts agreed on few things regarding mechanization with the exception of their expectation that mechanized forces would be used almost exclusively in an offensive role.

In general, the authors of these papers agreed that the Cavalry needed mechanized vehicles. Pierce went so far as to argue that mechanization would completely change warfare. He believed that the British Secretary of State for

Trooper Sam Silverman, 11th Cavalry Regiment, with his personal equipment laid out for inspection, *c*. 1930. (*USCM*)

War, Sir Laming Worthington-Evans, had correctly assessed the situation when he stated that:

> The additional mobility and carrying power of mechanical vehicles along with the striking force of tanks, are creating a revolution not in the principles of warfare, but in the application of those principles, just as the advent of motor traction has transformed the conduct of business life and even the social life of the nation.[16]

Pierce also concluded that in all traditional cavalry missions, mechanized cavalry performed as well as, if not better than, horse cavalry.[17]

In 1932, Major Wilson T. Bals, a cavalry officer, admitted that his attention was drawn to the number of mechanized vehicles then becoming more and more prevalent in the civilian world. Since American society was dominated by these vehicles, then, he asked, why should the Army not also be interested in them?[18] Bals believed that the high level of mobility of a mechanized cavalry regiment meant that it was wasted if attached to an infantry division. Therefore, he argued that such a regiment should be attached instead to a horse cavalry division.[19] The mechanized vehicles could keep up with and support horse cavalry, rather than outpacing the infantry. Bals also made what was a rather radical statement for the time: "That horse cavalry as heretofore armed, equipped and trained, cannot always perform with maximum efficiency, these [traditional] missions under modern conditions, is also generally agreed."[20]

In 1931, Major Adolphus W. Roffe, a cavalry officer, believed that international developments regarding mechanized forces made it necessary to develop similar forces.[21] Therefore, he understood mechanization to be driven by external, rather than internal or technological forces. Roffe also thought that the cavalry was the branch of the Army best suited to develop mobile forces.[22]

In 1936, through the use of charts and mathematical equations, Major Charles E. Dissinger, a cavalry officer, demonstrated that, on a soldier to soldier basis, a mechanized cavalry brigade had ten times the firepower per man as an infantry division and two times the firepower per man as a horse cavalry division.[23] With this in mind, Dissinger discussed three World War I battles during which mechanized cavalry could have provided a decisive advantage: the First Battle of Gaza in March 1917, the Battle of Megiddo in September 1917, and the Battle of Amiens in August 1918.[24] At Gaza, he envisioned that the mechanized cavalry's speed of maneuver would have allowed the British forces to capture the town before discovering that Turkish reinforcements were in route. In actuality, since the British had not consolidated their capture of Gaza, they withdrew rather than fight both the remaining forces in the town and the Turkish reinforcements.[25] At Megiddo, Dissinger argued for using mechanized cavalry as the "spearhead for the penetration or for the break-through of the enemy line."[26] The major effect of the addition of mechanized cavalry would have been to reduce infantry casualties since the battle was already a major British victory. At Amiens, Dissinger believed that the addition of mechanized cavalry with the British cavalry corps would have provided the shock action necessary to allow the cavalry to act independently of the slower infantry formations. Since the cavalry corps advanced 23 miles in reality, the addition of mechanized cavalry might have broken the entire German line in the Arras-Douai area.[27]

In addition to their agreement that the Cavalry needed mechanized vehicles, CGSS students also agreed that mechanized vehicles enhanced and supplemented, but should not replace, horse cavalry. For instance, Pierce compared the strengths and weaknesses of mechanized forces in the traditional roles of the cavalry. As a reconnaissance force, mechanized cavalry possessed greater range and the ability to break through enemy counter-reconnaissance easily (unless that enemy force was also mechanized) but could not perform close reconnaissance due to excessive noise. As a counter-reconnaissance force, mechanized cavalry overwhelmed any non-mechanized enemy but had difficulties with some types of terrain. As an offensive force, mechanized cavalry was most successful when the enemy was surprised in an undefended position but was less successful against an enemy armed with anti-tank weapons and/or in defensive positions. As a defensive force, Pierce saw mechanized cavalry as extremely limited, because it could not deploy as well as horse cavalry or infantry in defensive positions over a wide area. In exploiting a breakthrough and/or pursuit of an enemy force, mechanized cavalry was especially valuable, because its firepower and mobility allowed it take full

Horses Tricky and Gray held by African American troopers stationed at Fort Huachuca, Arizona, in 1939. (*LOC*)

advantage of the enemy's disarray. On raids, mechanized cavalry was very useful, but its relatively limited range (as compared to horse cavalry) made it vulnerable to becoming stranded and annihilated behind enemy lines.[28] Pierce believed that mechanized cavalry performed some roles better than horse cavalry, while the opposite was also true. However, since mechanized cavalry was so expensive to equip and maintain, it needed to be used selectively. As a result, he thought the two forms of cavalry should not be used interchangeably but rather adapted to perform the roles best suited to each.[29]

In his detailed discussion of the use of both mechanized and horse cavalry in reconnaissance, Curry illustrated the usual positive and negative characteristics of each type of cavalry. In light of those strengths and weaknesses, he advocated that mechanized cavalry was best suited for distant or "strategic" reconnaissance, while horse cavalry was more appropriate for close-in or tactical reconnaissance.[30] Likewise, Bonsteel, who believed that mechanized cavalry might do much to restore mobility to the battlefield, did not see it as a panacea. He believed that mechanized cavalry performed almost all of the traditional cavalry roles but was limited by terrain and logistical concerns. Senior officers, he advised, needed to understand how to employ mechanized cavalry properly or risk wasting it on unimportant missions.[31]

In 1930, Major Frank L. Whittaker, a cavalry officer, wrote that the greater range and speed of the armored car allowed the horse cavalry to remain rested for larger operations. In this way, the armored car complemented, rather than replaced, horse cavalry formations.[32] Similarly, in 1932, Major Lawrence C. Frizzell, another cavalry officer, did not believe the "extravagant claims" of many mechanized experts, who argued that both the horse cavalryman and the foot infantryman were already obsolete. Rather, he thought that, while mechanization changed the role of both the cavalry and infantry, it did not eliminate them—a proposition that was proved correct, at least for the infantry, by subsequent history.[33]

In 1932, Major Roy E. Blount, a cavalry officer, began his paper with the assumption that the Army could not completely mechanize and, therefore, mechanized forces would always serve as an auxiliary to the established combat branches.[34] He believed that mechanized cavalry would play a role in future warfare but, as with most other CGSS students, he thought that role would be subordinate to horse cavalry.[35] McNeill also agreed that mechanized cavalry had several abilities that made it superior to horse cavalry, but by and large, the mechanical unreliability of machines and necessity for greater logistical support made it merely a supplement to horse cavalry.[36]

The CGSS students also debated the tactical roles of horse and mechanized cavalry. During World War I, tanks operated under severe limitations and were ineffective unless supported by infantry. Interestingly, Dissinger proposed that horse cavalry more effectively supported tanks than infantry did, because horse cavalry was more mobile than infantry.[37] While horse cavalry was indeed more mobile than infantry, it was also more vulnerable due to the size of the horses. An infantryman could lay prone, enter a trench, or shell-hole for safety, but a horse had no such options. In addition, it was far easier for an infantryman to cross a "no-man's-land" than a man on horseback.

Whittaker argued that the armored car was to horse cavalry what horse cavalry was to the infantry. By which, he meant that the fast, maneuverable armored cars performed reconnaissance for the horse cavalry, just as the horse cavalry usually provided reconnaissance for the slower infantry formations.[38] Whittaker did not believe, however, that the role of the armored car was limited to reconnaissance. The armored car provided not only greater speed but also a platform for machine guns and larger weapons. Unfortunately, the principal advantage of the armored car—speed—was lost if the armored car was employed in direct coordination with horse cavalry or infantry formations. Therefore, according to Whittaker, the armored car, while ideally a part of the cavalry, needed to operate independently of horse cavalry formations.[39]

Nevertheless, other CGSS students refused to believe that mechanized forces were capable of acting independently of horses. Roffe did not foresee a time in the immediate future when mechanized forces could operate independently of horse cavalry.[40] Pierce agreed and believed that it was combined-arms formations that were most effective in warfare and, therefore, mechanized forces were merely another part of that larger mosaic.[41]

Some of the CGSS students also discussed how to organize mechanized forces within the cavalry. Pierce believed that one mechanized cavalry regiment was necessary for each cavalry division, which allowed the division to provide the administrative and logistical support necessary for the regiment.[42] Roffe discussed whether the then current organization of cavalry divisions was satisfactory or required improvement. At the time, the organization of cavalry units was based more on decisions made within the Congress rather than the needs of the Army.[43] Roffe provided nine pages of specific organizational problems and his thoughts on their most obvious solutions. Among Roffe's recommendations were: the need to reorganize Army divisions around three maneuver regiments to replace the previous organization of two maneuver brigades (each containing two maneuver regiments) per division; the discontinuation of the tanks then assigned to the cavalry, since they were too slow and had too little maneuverability; the addition of a third battalion of field artillery; the replacement of wire communications with radios; additional trucks to replace motorcycles and horse-drawn transportation; the addition of more .30- and .50-caliber machine guns; the addition of an armored car platoon at the regimental level; the replacement of the Springfield Model 1903 rifle with a semi-automatic weapon; the retention of the saber for ceremonial purposes only; and the addition of a mechanized regiment in each division.[44]

Curry concluded that the size of mechanized cavalry reconnaissance formations needed to be a brigade at the army level, a regiment at the corps level, and a squadron at the division level. In contrast, the size of horse cavalry reconnaissance formations needed to be a division at the army level, a brigade at the corps level,

Annual cavalry endurance test, Fort Riley, Kansas, September 24, 1924. (*LOC*)

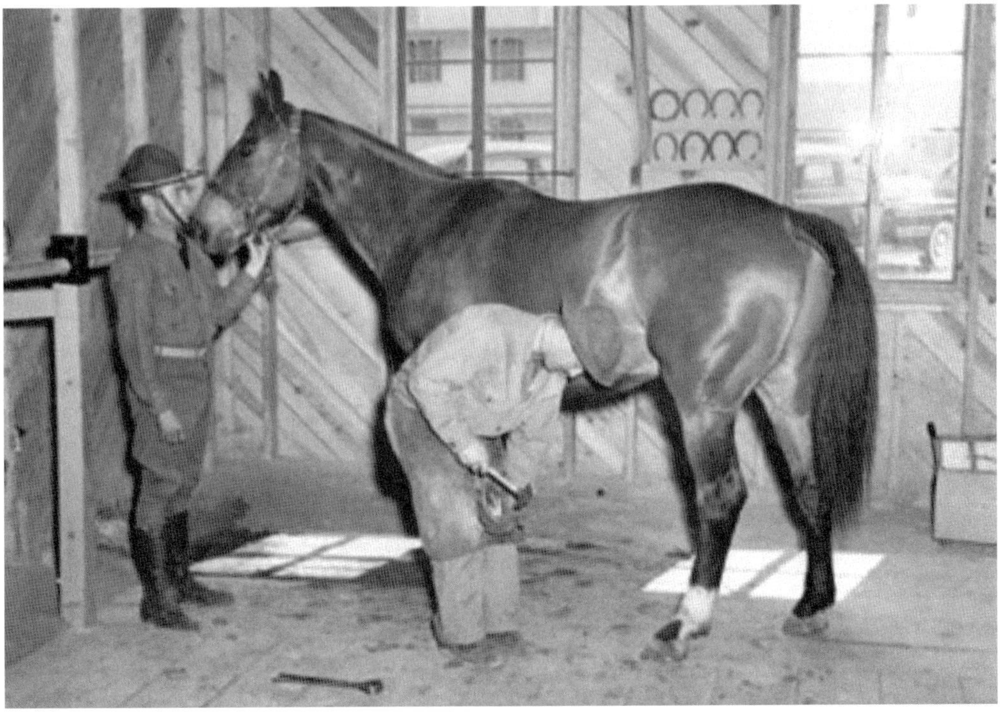

Farrier shoeing a horse, Cavalry School, Fort Riley, Kansas, 1941. (*USCM*)

and a regiment at the division level.[45] In short, Curry believed that both types of cavalry were necessary to perform proper reconnaissance but that the firepower and strength of mechanized cavalry reduced the size of the necessary force.

Blount proposed that there were only three appropriate places to locate mechanized forces within the cavalry—integrated into all cavalry formations, as a part of the cavalry division, or as General Headquarters reserve force for use in major turning movements, distant pursuit, or deep raids.[46] He dismissed the notion of integrating mechanized cavalry into horse cavalry formations because this greatly complicated supply and training with little actual gain in combat effectiveness. Likewise, mechanized cavalry used only as a General Headquarters reserve force would find it difficult to coordinate operations with horse cavalry formations in combat. The most logical option, in his opinion, was to integrate mechanized cavalry as part of the cavalry division organizational structure.[47]

With this organization, the cavalry division provided the administrative and logistical support to mechanized cavalry. Also, since any mechanized cavalry would most likely operate in support of horse cavalry, it was best located within the cavalry division. Nevertheless, this arrangement did not prevent the mechanized cavalry from being detached for special operations on behalf of the General Headquarters. In addition, Blount agreed with other CGSS students who believed that mechanized cavalry needed to be either a regiment or an entire brigade of each cavalry division.[48]

Some of the CGSS students attempted to justify the inclusion of mechanized forces within the historical traditions of the cavalry. Frizzell stated that the principal characteristics of the cavalry had always been, and would always be, mobility and firepower. Mechanized cavalry simply changed the means by which mobility occurred and the manner in which the firepower was transported.[49] McNeill agreed that mechanized cavalry was a welcome and useful addition to the cavalry branch and did not create a major break with the horse cavalry's traditional roles on the battlefield.[50]

While the cavalry had, by and large, abandoned shock action by the latter part of the nineteenth century, as modern weaponry made those actions far too costly in men and horses, both Blount and Dissinger went so far as to argue that mechanization was a possible method of restoring shock value to cavalry.[51] Dissinger believed that modern warfare lacked shock action and that the reestablishment of shock action was important. He began by defining shock action as the use of cavalry to overwhelm the enemy by impact alone, or as he quoted German Field Marshall Count Alfred von Schlieffen—"annihilation."[52] Then Dissinger provided historical examples of the use of cavalry shock action from the eighteenth and nineteenth centuries as well as from World War I.[53] The two World War I examples he provided were of a rather dubious nature: the capture of Beersheba by the Australian 4th Light Horse Brigade in October 1917 and the British 6th Cavalry Brigade at Villeselve, France, in March 1918. The success of both of these attacks was due primarily to luck. In the case of the Beersheba attack, the Ottoman defenders had incorrectly sighted their rifles so that they

Cavalry unit being reviewed in 1927. (*LOC*)

were shooting above the heads of the rapidly advancing Australians. In the case of Villeselve, the German soldiers, who were dispirited after almost four years of trench warfare, found themselves exposed in the open rather than entrenched in a defensive position. Dissinger admitted that the examples of cavalry shock action during World War I were the exceptions rather than the rule. He then discussed the successful use of tanks during World War I and concluded that they were the best method of restoring shock to the battlefield.

Discussions of technological improvements demonstrate that CGSS students accepted mechanized vehicles as a part of the cavalry. They took these vehicles for granted and debated only how many and what type of mechanized vehicles to use. Roffe proposed discontinuing the tanks assigned to the cavalry because they were too slow and had too little maneuverability.[54] By and large, the tanks used in 1931 were not dissimilar to the tanks used during World War I. These tanks traveled at extremely slow speeds, had a short range, and were prone to frequent breakdowns. Roffe did not oppose mechanization by proposing the discontinuation of these tanks; rather, he promoted furthering mechanization by replacing inappropriate technology with vehicles which, he hoped, better served the cavalry's function. Indeed, Roffe proposed adding an armored car platoon to each cavalry regiment.[55] The platoon would be part of the regimental headquarters troop and provide reconnaissance for the entire regiment. Roffe believed that his recommendation was in keeping with the mechanized developments of both the Army and American society. Since tanks were still far too slow to be used for reconnaissance, his proposal was the best possible option at the time.

Sergeant Frank W. Smith, one of the best horsemen of Troop F, 3rd Cavalry Regiment, jumps over a human bar composed of the arms of two fellow troopers at Fort Myer, Virginia. (*LOC*)

Taking into consideration the traditional roles of cavalry forces, Bals proposed that five different mechanized vehicles were needed by the cavalry. The first of these vehicles was a heavy, tracked "combat car" capable of cross-country movement and equipped with either two machines guns or one machine gun and a light gun. The second type of vehicle was a light, tracked "combat car" also capable of cross-country movement, but having lighter weight, greater speed, and only one machine gun. The third type of vehicle was a light armored car for reconnaissance. The fourth type of vehicle was a weapons carrier capable of carrying a squad or more of cavalrymen cross-country in support of the "combat cars." The fifth and final type of vehicle was a light truck used primarily to transport supplies. Bals believed that the large number of vehicles that this formation required and their diverse roles necessitated that any mechanized cavalry formation be of at least regimental size.[56] While at first inspection, Bals' mechanized cavalry regiment might appear to have too many different types of vehicles, a closer examination explains these proposals. The overriding principle of military technological development has always been that weapons were developed to suit the mission, rather than the opposite. As a result, Bals did not attempt to change the military missions to suit only one or two types of vehicles, but rather, he wished to develop different vehicles to perform different missions.

Pair of ambulances from the 10th Cavalry Regiment at Fort Huachuca, Arizona, in 1918. (*LOC*)

The vehicles required for an effective mechanized cavalry force had to possess a combination of mobility, firepower, and armored protection. With those attributes in mind, Frizzell believed that, though those qualities might all be necessary, they were also frequently contradictory. For instance, though mobility and armored protection were both necessary, they also worked against one another. More armored protection also meant more weight and, therefore, less mobility.[57]

According to these CGSS students, several types of vehicles were necessary for the mechanized cavalry to perform effectively. Frizzell separated these vehicles by mission—reconnaissance and engagement. The vehicles used for reconnaissance needed to emphasize mobility over both firepower and armored protection. He assumed that armored cars were best for performing the reconnaissance role. For engagement, he believed that a convertible vehicle capable of riding on tracks for off-road operations and riding on wheels for on-road operations was ideal. Since that type of vehicle had not been perfected, however, he proposed using a heavy "combat car" of the Christie type (Model 1928) for engagement purposes. Though the Christie was a prototype in many ways, and had not yet been formally accepted by the Army, Frizzell believed that it was a step in the right direction.[58] As with several other CGSS students, Frizzell believed that more than one type of vehicle was necessary to perform cavalry missions. This, yet again, reflects the desire to make the vehicle conform to the mission, rather than the other way around.

On the topic of the design of armored car needed by the Army, Whittaker evaluated the types of armored cars then available and commented on the advantages and disadvantages of each. Only one type of heavy armored car, the Christie Model 1928, had been tested by the Army. Though the Christie is generally classified as a tank, Whittaker considered it an armored car because its tracks were removable and it could be driven on hard-rubber wheels. The Model 1928 had a great many advantages, including convertibility and maneuverability. Nevertheless, Whittaker believed that the Army was better served by developing the Model 1928 into a tank to replace the slow and less maneuverable tanks of the time. He also reasoned that the relatively large size of the Model 1928 made it unsuited for use as an armored car.[59]

The medium armored car then in the Army arsenal was designed on a La Salle automobile chassis, which was actually a division of General Motors. The La Salle had the advantages of greater road mobility than the Christie and ease of production due to its commercial chassis. The disadvantages were its large size and, since it was based on a commercial chassis, its lack of ruggedness. Though at the time no light armored car was part of the Army's arsenal, Whittaker discussed the experiments then underway to design just such a vehicle. Theoretically, the light armored car would have two principal advantages—its small size and weight, which made it both more mobile and less visible as a target. Whittaker listed no disadvantages to this type of armored car.[60]

In his conclusions, Whittaker dismissed the medium type of armored car as offering no real advantages over the Christie or the light armored car. Of the two remaining armored cars, he believed that the light type more easily performed the traditional cavalry missions, while also being more economical and easier to produce. At the same time, Whittaker recommended developing the Christie further and eventually replacing all of the tanks in cavalry formations.[61] Interestingly, a light armored car of the type described by Whittaker ultimately saw wide use by the Army during World War II. That vehicle, the M9 Greyhound, was a lightly armed and armored vehicle capable of rapid advance on and off-road, which was frequently used in a reconnaissance role.

In 1936, Captain George T. Barnes, a quartermaster officer, examined the different reconnaissance roles of aircraft and armored cars as well as the strengths and weaknesses of each. Aviation was capable of reconnaissance far in advance of the main force but was limited by weather conditions and terrain. In addition, the level of detail provided by aviation reconnaissance was minimal in comparison with mechanized cavalry. While also limited by terrain, mechanized cavalry provided far more detailed reconnaissance than aviation.[62] Barnes made two recommendations regarding cavalry division organization. He believed that an aviation squadron and a mechanized cavalry squadron were needed in the organization of each cavalry division for use by the division commander on reconnaissance missions.[63] Tellingly, Barnes never discussed the use of horse cavalry in the reconnaissance role.

Trooper of the 12th Cavalry Regiment, *c.* 1921. (*USCM*)

As the preceding pages demonstrated, CGSS students writing on mechanization gave a great deal of thought to the question of mechanization and the future of the cavalry. Most of the student papers on this topic envisioned a greater role for the future of mechanization than was official Army policy at the time. The fact that even cavalry officers discussed these possibilities demonstrated that these officers were "pragmatic" regarding the possible future of mechanized forces in the Cavalry and the Army as a whole.

Senior officer of the 12th Cavalry Regiment, *c.* 1920. (*USCM*)

6

"Compromiser": Patton's Approach to Mechanization

In addition to the "traditionalists," "modernizers," and "pragmatists," one interwar cavalry officer—George S. Patton, Jr.—carved his own unique position. Patton was unique because rather than being indifferent or remaining silent, he was vocally supportive of both sides in the debate between horses and mechanization. Perhaps Patton represents another response—the "compromiser" reaction to mechanization.

For a man who is often regarded as one of the masters of armored warfare, George S. Patton, Jr., was decidedly ambivalent about cavalry mechanization. Unlike contemporary military innovators such as Giulio Douhet, J. F. C. Fuller, Sir Basil H. Liddell Hart, and Billy Mitchell, Patton was unwilling to risk his career despite his World War I service with the Tank Corps and continued support for new technology.[1] This ambivalent response challenges popular images of a headstrong, single-minded Patton, suggesting a personality in which the "traditionalist" increasingly contended with the "modernizer."

Patton was born in San Gabriel, California, on November 11, 1885, to a family that had a long history of military/public service. John Mercer Patton (his great-grandfather) served as the governor of Virginia, while George S. Patton (his grandfather) was killed in action while commanding the Confederate 22nd Virginia Infantry Regiment at the Battle of Opequon on September 19, 1864. In 1904, after a year at the Virginia Military Institute, Patton received an appointment to the United States Military Academy. A mediocre to poor student (he was forced to repeat his freshman year), he excelled in the "soldierly" aspects of the West Point experience. His standing at West Point improved to the point that during his senior year, he was named the cadet adjutant, a title awarded to "the cadet who exemplified soldierly conduct and who had demonstrated the ability to command and to impose discipline."[2]

After graduating in 1909, Patton was commissioned a second lieutenant in the 15th Cavalry Regiment and served at Fort Sheridan, Illinois, and then Fort Myer, Virginia, until 1912. He was a member of the U.S. Olympic team at the 1912

Fox and dog mascots of a troop in the 12th Cavalry Regiment. (*USCM*)

The full kit of a cavalry trooper, *c.* 1916. (*USCM*)

Summer Games in Stockholm, Sweden, where he finished fifth in the Modern Pentathlon. Between 1913 and 1915, Patton was simultaneously an instructor in swordsmanship and a student at the Cavalry School, Fort Riley, Kansas. While stationed at Fort Riley, he designed a new saber (the last combat saber ever issued by the U.S. Army) to replace the model that had been largely unchanged since before the Civil War.[3]

During the Mexican Punitive Expedition in 1916, Patton served as an aide to the Expedition's commander, Brigadier General John J. Pershing. On May 14, 1916, while on a mission to purchase grain, Patton was confronted by and forced to battle three Villista soldiers at a Mexican ranch. Though he was accompanied by ten cavalrymen, Patton personally wounded one and killed the other two Villistas. One of the Villistas killed during the "battle," Colonel Julio Cárdanas, was a senior advisor of General Francisco "Pancho" Villa. Patton was personally commended by Pershing for his bravery and initiative during the incident. On May 23, the *New York Times* ran a story on Patton's "battle," and the author of the article noted that it was a new type of combat because Patton and his men arrived not on horseback but in automobiles. The reporter was correct, this represented the first example of motorized warfare in American history.[4] Through his pre-World War I accomplishments, therefore, Patton established himself as a "hell for leather"-type cavalry officer. However, it was his World War I experiences that left the most indelible impression on the remainder of his military career.

First Lieutenant George S. Patton, Jr., in Mexico during the Punitive Expedition on June 10, 1916. (*LOC*)

Following the American declaration of war against the Central Powers in April 1917, Pershing was appointed the commander of the American Expeditionary Forces (AEF), and he chose Patton to be the commander of the headquarters company for the entire AEF. After serving in this position for his first six months in France, Patton requested and was granted a transfer to the newly organized Tank Corps. In fact, he was the very first officer assigned to the Tank Corps.[5] The reason for his transfer request appears to have been twofold. First, he was tired of his "desk job," which, though difficult and rigorous, seemed a poor substitute for the combat command that he so desperately wanted. Second, he did not want to serve as an infantry or field artillery officer and horse cavalry had seen almost no combat since 1914, which made the Tank Corps his only viable option if he wished to serve in combat.

Between November 1917 and August 1918, Patton was promoted to lieutenant colonel as well as organized and commanded the Light Tank Center and School at Langres, France. He relinquished command of the Light Tank Center just in time to lead the newly organized 304th Tank Brigade during the Battle of Saint-Mihiel (September 12–16, 1918). Already well-known for his personal bravery, Patton led his tanks into combat on foot, since he believed that it was impossible to command his troops from the inside of a tank. In order to "lead from the front," Patton left the safety of his command post, which was also his link to higher headquarters. The American First Army achieved its designated objectives during the battle and the most resistance that the tankers encountered was from their equipment and a shortage of gasoline. After the battle, however, Brigadier General Samuel D. Rockenbach, the commander of the AEF Tank Corps, reprimanded Patton for his failure to remain with his headquarters. Rockenbach believed that Patton should have stayed at his command post to coordinate the actions of his unit with the orders of higher headquarters.[6] Patton, on the other hand, argued that an officer should lead by example. While Patton's approach certainly achieved its objectives, it could come at a high cost as he discovered on his return to combat.

On the first day of the Meuse-Argonne Offensive (September 26, 1918), Patton grew impatient after the first hour of the battle at the 304th Tank Brigade headquarters and decided to venture onto the battlefield. With only a half-dozen or so men, he reached the frontline and almost immediately came under fire from German machine guns. Forced to take cover behind a small hill, Patton began assembling a force of American infantrymen, most of whom had become separated from their units. After approximately 100 men had joined him, Patton led them forward in support of his tanks. As they advanced over open ground, Patton was wounded by a bullet that entered his upper left thigh, passed through his body, and exited his left buttock. Despite profuse bleeding, he refused to be evacuated. While wounded and in an exposed position, Patton continued to direct the actions of his tankers until they neutralized twenty-five German machine-gun nests and advanced out of sight. After being carried to safety, he insisted on being driven to the U.S. 35th Division headquarters to report on the conditions at the

Colonel George S. Patton, Jr., posing in front of an FT17 tank during World War I. (*NARA*)

front. The 304th Tank Brigade, which had begun the Meuse-Argonne Offensive with 141 tanks, remained on the frontline until October 16, 1918, by which time it had only twenty operational tanks.[7] While recuperating from his wound in a French hospital, Patton was promoted to colonel and then, a few days after the Armistice on November 11, 1918, awarded the Distinguished Service Cross, the U.S. Army's second highest decoration for heroism.[8]

On June 30, 1920, Patton was discharged from the National Army with the rank of colonel in the Tank Corps and reverted to his Regular Army rank of captain in the cavalry.[9] A month later, he was promoted to major but had only two real career options. Patton could remain with tanks, which meant transferring to the infantry, or he could abandon tanks and return to the horse cavalry. He chose to return to the cavalry, a branch where he was well-known and more likely to advance along a normal career path.[10] Arguably, if Patton had been as supportive of tanks as he would later claim, then he should have remained with tanks even if it meant a branch transfer. Therefore, his decision to leave tanks was a decision based on a desire for career advancement.

In order to determine Patton's opinions on mechanization and the future of the horse during the interwar period, his lectures, personal correspondence, official reports, and *Cavalry Journal* articles are undoubtedly the best source of

Officers of the 3rd Cavalry Regiment at Fort Myer, Virginia. Then-Major George S. Patton, Jr., can be seen bared-headed third row from the bottom. (*USCM*)

information. In preparing the after-action report of the 304th Tank Brigade in the Meuse-Argonne Offensive, Patton proposed nine "Tactical Conclusions." Three of the nine centered on the infantry. He believed that infantrymen did not understand that tanks could not operate independently and required infantry support in order to be successful. At the same time, however, the infantry on occasion halted and waited for tanks before advancing. This was a mistake because the mechanical unreliability of the tank meant that it could never be depended upon. Indeed, the mechanical unreliability of tanks, combined with their firepower and mobility, meant that they should always be employed *en masse*. Patton also believed that it was important to reduce the distance between the line of departure and the battlefield due to the tanks' mechanical unreliability. Lastly, he urged commanders to perform a thorough preliminary reconnaissance of the battlefield on foot before deploying tanks.[11] Patton saw the importance of the tank and hoped to impart his ideas to Army officers who had no experience with tanks during World War I.

In a lecture to the American General Staff College in France on November 23, 1918, Patton stated that tanks were the last word in shock troops, the modern equivalent of the Greek hoplite, the Carthaginian elephant, or the medieval knight.[12] In another lecture on December 5, 1918, Patton toyed with the notion of deep penetration of enemy lines by tanks. Though an interesting notion, he knew that it was physically impossible at that time, since tanks required refueling after relatively short distances.[13] Soon after the Armistice, Patton began working on a manuscript that eventually numbered twenty-six singled-spaced pages and presented his views on warfare and patriotism. The most interesting portion of this manuscript was his statement that:

> In wars without such flankless lines penetrations or encircling movements by cavalry and tanks will, I believe, be sufficient to break up to a large degree the great gun concentrations and thus permit moving fire and force to gain decisive results.[14]

Therefore, Patton believed that it was a combination of horses and tanks, rather than either one independently, which would restore mobility to the battlefield following the stalemate of the Western Front during World War I.

In April 1919, Patton received a letter from a board of cavalry officers that was surveying other cavalry officers on their opinions regarding horse cavalry tactics, armament, organization, and the horse's utility in future warfare. Most of Patton's responses in regards to the future use of the cavalry were directed toward a conflict with or in Mexico. He also made rather specific recommendations regarding the use of new weaponry in the cavalry:

> He recommended that the newly developed air-cooled machine gun replace the water-cooled barrel, that the number of automatic rifles in a cavalry division be increased drastically, that the Stokes mortar be added to cavalry squadrons, and that the saber be retained to stimulate "morale and dash."[15, 16]

In addition, it is noteworthy that he mentioned that horse cavalry should concentrate its operations in terrain that was impassable to armored cars and tanks. Lastly, he betrayed his indecision about his own future in the Army by signing his response, "Col. Tank Corps (Maj. Cav.)."[17] Patton's command of a tank brigade during World War I had clearly had an effect on his opinions regarding the future role of horse cavalry.

Further complicating his position on horses *versus* mechanized vehicles, Patton played a role in the development of mechanized technology. In April 1919, Patton was appointed to the Army Tank Board, whose purpose was to formulate tank regulations as well as prepare a drill manual and a course of instruction for tankers.[18] He was very active on this board, as well as independently, in discussing, examining, and proposing changes and improvements to both tanks and tank doctrine. As a member of the Tank Board, Patton was present for the demonstration of the Christie Model 1919 chassis. Even this early model of the Christie chassis was extremely innovative. The Model 1919 was the first tank chassis in which the entire machine and each major component part thereof had been designed and constructed solely for use as a military vehicle.[19] The excellent performance of the chassis during the tests led the Tank Board to conclude that the Army should purchase the Model 1919 for further testing. Though the Ordnance Department, which had the final approval in development of all weapons, was

Sergeant of the 12th Cavalry Regiment at Fort Riley, Kansas. (*USCM*)

hesitant to purchase Christie's chassis, Patton wrote a strongly worded letter in support of the design, and his comments were seconded by Rockenbach. Unfortunately, on the recommendation of the AEF's Superior Board and with the support of Pershing, tanks were re-designated as an infantry support weapon.[20, 21] The Superior Board's recommendation had a serious effect on tank development following the passage of the National Defense Act of 1920 because tanks were relegated to the infantry and tank mechanical development continued to be the exclusive purview of the Ordnance Department.

In a September 1919 lecture to the Tank School at Camp Meade, Maryland, Patton stated unequivocally that tanks were an auxiliary offensive weapon. They neither could nor should operate independently of infantry or in a defensive capacity. Likewise, he believed that the best defense against enemy tanks was provided not by artillery but by other tanks. Since the concept of anti-tank formations had not yet been completely formulated, artillery was usually the greatest enemy of tanks during World War I.[22] In Patton's opinion, tank battles in the future would resemble naval battles, as large, heavily armored machines engaged one another over long distances.[23] Patton was one of the few individuals who early on envisioned tank *versus* tank battles. Most other officers believed that tanks would be engaged by artillery or anti-tank weapons rather than other tanks.

Patton's position as an expert in tank warfare resulted in his being consulted by other officers. For example, in 1921, Major Bradford G. Chynoweth, who had worked in the civilian automotive industry before becoming an infantry tank officer after World War I, sent an article on the topic of "Cavalry Tanks"

Brigadier General Samuel D. Rockenbach, Chief of Tank Corps in World War I, at Chaumont, France, on September 5, 1918. (*LOC*)

to Patton for his comments. In his article, Chynoweth claimed that modern warfare owed more to national economies and technological development than it did to individual heroics—the mass-produced machine gun in World War I being the best example of this notion. He believed that nations entered World War I with more men than they knew how to properly employ on the battlefield and fewer machines than they required. The result of this miscalculation, or perhaps misunderstanding of the changes in warfare, was the bloodbath on the Western Front.[24]

Chynoweth demanded that his readers recognize that mechanized vehicles were not going away just because the U.S. Army failed to appreciate their value in warfare. On the contrary, he believed that these vehicles continued to improve technologically and would dominate future battlefields. Chynoweth, who was not a cavalry officer, clearly recognized that cavalry was a concept rather than a man on a horse. If the economic and technological situations improved, he believed much, if not most, of the cavalry would be mechanized to allow it to remain an effective branch of the Army.[25]

Patton's reply was reprinted in a slightly edited version immediately following Chynoweth's article in the *Cavalry Journal*. Patton took issue with what he believed was Chynoweth's "picture of a senile and impotent [horse] cavalry, futilely butting its head against impregnable strong points."[26] Patton believed that the situation in France during World War I was unique in respect to the fixed flanks of the frontlines. He was convinced that in any other situation horse cavalry would have found and turned the enemy's flanks, thus deciding the conflict.

In addition, Patton noted that horse cavalry operated on independent raids during which supply lines were unnecessary, while tanks were closely tied to supply lines for gas, oil, and spare parts. He readily admitted that in other actions, such as counterattacks and short turning movements, tanks were invaluable, but these actions were of a limited nature. Patton then argued that the national industrial capacity was incapable of producing enough tanks to replace the horse in combat. This attitude regarding industrial capacity was a common theme of most interwar Army officers, regardless of their branch of service or point of view on the issue of mechanization. Patton also believed that, in certain terrains, such as the mountains of northern Mexico, the rice paddies of the Philippines, and the forests of Canada, the tank was relatively useless. Despite these criticisms, however, he defined himself as "enthusiastic a tanker as ever caterpillared" and stated that the tank was "a special, technical, and vastly powerful weapon."[27] Patton ended his remarks by

Troopers of the 12th Cavalry Regiment grooming a horse. (*USCM*)

stating that an independent Tank Corps was necessary to properly develop and coordinate tanks with the existing combat arms. In one article, then, he managed both to defend the horse cavalry and to advocate an independent Tank Corps.

In April 1922, another of Patton's articles defended the usefulness of both horses and tanks in evaluating the effect of World War I on horse cavalry. Patton began by reiterating his comments regarding the uniqueness of the Western Front during World War I. The unique aspects were the fixed flanks, which prevented horse cavalry from maneuvering properly, and the extensive rail and road network on both sides, which permitted the concentration of men and ammunition.[28] Patton then pointed out that different circumstances had existed both on the Eastern Front and in the Middle East, where horse cavalry saw extensive use. In Palestine, for instance, out of a total of thirty-four mounted cavalry charges, only two were unsuccessful.[29] In all of these circumstances, however, he believed that the main point was to concentrate the greatest number of men and armaments in order to achieve a major breakthrough or turn the enemy's flank. For Patton, this notion was best expressed by Confederate Lieutenant General Nathan Bedford Forrest's often quoted maxim, "Getting there fust with the mostest men."[30]

Patton acknowledged that several technological developments during World War I had forever altered warfare. The airplane and the tank were, in his opinion, the most significant of these developments. Patton believed that the airplane changed the definition of "good cavalry country." While cavalrymen previously thought that large, open spaces, such as the prairie of the American West, were ideal for the use of cavalry, the invention of the airplane made those spaces entirely too vulnerable to aerial reconnaissance. According to Patton, the airplane changed the desired countryside for the cavalry from grasslands to woodlands, where the cavalry was able to use the cover of the trees to screen their movements.[31]

The stalemate of the Western Front was, Patton believed, the result of a lack of understanding in the use of horse cavalry: "High authority is of the opinion that the German failure to use their mounted arm at Artois and on the Marne probably cost them, if not decisive, at least great strategic, successes."[32] Likewise, he believed that the machine gun, rather than spelling the end of the horse cavalry, actually gave the cavalry the dismounted firepower that they so long desired. Patton stated that both tanks and horse cavalry were suited to specific types of terrain and operations and, therefore, needed to be used accordingly. He identified the six tactical operations in which horse cavalry was most useful: delaying or harassing action against infantry; attacks against flanks or thinly held sectors; actions against enemy cavalry; action against enemy lines of communication; actions by patrols; and actions against strong positions, where either cover or obstacles prevent maneuver.[33] All of these were tactical operations of a basically offensive nature, while the last of these was performed dismounted and only as a last resort. Again, in this article, Patton defended both horse cavalry and tanks, maintaining that each has its role on the battlefield.

In 1924, Patton again attempted to reconcile horse and tank warfare by advocating coordination between horse and mechanized cavalry. In particular,

Sergeant Holden of Troop B, 9th Cavalry Regiment, instructs recruits on the use of the air-cooled M1919A2 machine gun. (*USCM*)

this article discussed the possibility of using armored cars in support of horse cavalry formations. Patton began by presenting a fictional account of an entirely mechanized future battle. Ironically, though he meant the fictional account to be taken tongue-in-cheek, in many ways it can be compared to the late twentieth- or early twenty-first-century American way of war. Tank-killing aircraft, observation helicopters, long-range command and control centers, and fast moving (50 mph) tanks that were sealed against chemical warfare, had video screens, and communicated with each other and their commanders via radio were all present in Patton's "farce." He posited the question, "Shall such battles occur?," which he answered that given past experiences, it was a "bold" man who would deny the possibility.[34] Patton then criticized both those who believed that such battles were just around the corner and those who denied that any fundamental change had occurred in warfare. He labeled both groups as "insane."[35]

Endeavoring to "separate facts from fiction," Patton then discussed what he believed was one of the historical absolutes of warfare—the importance of logistics. Without supplies, no army could maintain operations for very long, and terrain was a crucial part of this equation. As Patton pointed out, even with every truck in the AEF, General Ulysses S. Grant could not have done a much better job of supplying his troops during the Battle of the Wilderness due to the terrain.[36] Technology had changed, however, and instead of wheeled vehicles that were closely tied to roads, newer vehicles with caterpillar treads were no longer so restricted. Though these tracked vehicles offered many advantages, Patton believed that technology and finance prevented the wide-spread use of them. The mechanical reliability of these vehicles was also greatly in doubt and the traditionally parsimonious American government was unlikely to produce the necessary funds to procure them in sufficient numbers.

As a result of the lack of sufficient technology and financial means, Patton abandoned the idea of tanks for the cavalry. In their place, though not their equal in many respects, was the armored car. The type of armored car that Patton discussed was a lightly armored vehicle (capable of stopping rifle fire at 100 yards) built around a commercial truck chassis (for ease in acquiring spare parts), which mounted one air-cooled machine-gun.[37] Since the British had used similar vehicles with great success during World War I, Patton believed that such vehicles had already proved their worth. These vehicles would not replace traditional cavalry formations but were suitable in many traditional cavalry roles when the terrain was appropriate. Patton recommended that between a platoon and a squadron of men in each cavalry regiment be equipped with these armored cars to add both mobility and firepower.[38] Four years later, a smaller form of his recommendation was enacted, when an armored car troop was attached to the 1st Cavalry Division, at Fort Bliss, Texas.[39] Yet again, Patton wrote seeking a compromise between horses and tanks.

Interestingly, an article Patton co-authored with Major Clarence C. Benson took a surprising view of the coordination between horse and mechanized forces. Patton and Benson were the cavalry representatives on a board appointed to evaluate the trials of the Christie Model 1928 chassis and the performance of the chassis had an effect on both of the authors. They began the article by stating that horse cavalry now faced perhaps the greatest threat to its existence—mechanization. Patton and Benson took a defensive tone against mechanization by beginning with a list of World War I general officers who continued to support horse cavalry. The authors believed that all branches of the Army, combat and non-combat, were affected by mechanization, but the result for the cavalry was even more significant than the other branches. Patton and Benson also included the oft-repeated weaknesses of mechanized vehicles, such as supply limitations, control difficulties, and terrain problems.[40]

Patton and Benson argued that the infantry and the cavalry needed to develop different kinds of vehicles to fulfill markedly different roles. The infantry needed heavily armored tanks but did not require high speed because they only had to be fast enough to accompany and support infantry advancing on foot. The cavalry, on the other hand, required fast cross-country machines capable of keeping up with and supporting horse cavalry formations.[41] Patton and Benson also discussed the possibilities offered by mechanized vehicles operating in coordination with horse cavalry formations. These possibilities included protecting horse cavalry against enemy aircraft and mechanized vehicles, reconnaissance and offensive action over open ground, counter-reconnaissance, flank and rear guard duty, delaying actions, and actions in breakthroughs.[42] Patton and Benson cautioned their audience (other cavalry officers) that motorized vehicles could not be ignored: "To bury

Above left: Private First Class Thomas Hawker, Troop H, 9th Cavalry Regiment. Hawker was the first trooper from the 9th Cavalry to be on the Chief of Cavalry's Rifle Team for marksmanship, *c.* 1924. (*USCM*)

Above right: Technical Sergeant Frank Lang, Headquarters Troop, 8th Cavalry, Fort Bliss, Texas, 1931. (*USCM*)

Trooper of the 7th Cavalry Regiment in the field at Fort Riley, Kansas. (*USCM*)

our heads, ostrich-like, and ignore [mechanized vehicles], would be foolish."[43] Nevertheless, they were convinced that the cavalry could ultimately adapt to the new circumstances on the battlefield: "If the 14th Century knight could adapt himself to gunpowder, we should have no fear of oil, grease, and motors."[44] In the end, Patton and Benson advocated cooperation between tanks and the existing combat branches, rather than the creation of a separate branch.

The article's conclusion was curious, since Patton argued several years earlier for the recreation of an independent Tank Corps. It is possible that Patton changed his mind as a result of the major technological developments that had occurred since World War I. These technological developments made tanks more than just lumbering 5-mph contraptions. However, this does not completely explain the turnabout in Patton's thinking. Another possible motivation was that, while in 1921 Patton envisioned both an independent tank corps and an independent cavalry branch, in 1930 he may have believed that an independent tank corps with Christie-type mechanized vehicles completely usurped the cavalry's functions. Patton seemed comfortable with the notion of both horses and tanks existing simultaneously, but possibly he could not conceive of a cavalry completely devoid of horses. This notion was supported by comments he made immediately after World War II in which, even at that late date, Patton supported retaining a limited amount of horse cavalry.

In 1932, Patton, while a student at the Army War College, prepared a paper on the characteristics of future warfare and the organization, tactics, and equipment that the Army required. The thesis of Patton's paper was that throughout history armies varied between those based on quantity and those based on quality. His purpose was to examine this historical trend and determine which type of army was preferable for the United States.[45] Patton discussed quite a few different issues in this essay, but the most important of these were his ideas regarding the composition of the future U.S. Army. He believed that the Army did not possess enough mechanized or motorized vehicles. Though he did not advocate completely mechanizing the Army, he did believe that it required more vehicles than it then possessed. In particular, he was convinced that the Army needed more trucks to transport supplies.[46]

Patton advocated the complete reorganization of the infantry around a light, air-cooled .30-caliber machine gun. Oddly enough, Patton's infantry organization was very similar to that used by the German Army during World War II. In addition, he believed that all infantry units from the squad to the division needed restructuring. The result was a divisional structure that most closely resembled that utilized by the U.S. Army from the early 1960s to the early twenty-first century. Lastly, he wanted to reorganize horse cavalry along the same lines as the infantry, but with an expansion of mechanized cavalry.[47] Patton envisioned a significantly larger and more heavily mechanized and motorized Army. While he did not specifically advocate the reduction of horses and mules in the Army, the implication of his request for more motorized and mechanized vehicles would have resulted in a reduction of horse and mules. Therefore, combined with the reorganization of all infantry and cavalry units, the Army organization that

Members of the tent pegging team, 7th Cavalry Regiment, Fort Riley, Kansas. (*USCM*)

Patton advocated in 1932 resembled the organization of the Army that fought from Vietnam to the beginning of the War on Terror.

In 1933, Patton evaluated the usefulness of mechanized forces in a lecture delivered to the Army War College. He began by once again presenting the reasons that he believed it was impossible to repeat the strategic situation in Europe during World War I. Patton then proceeded to list the advantages and disadvantages of mechanized forces. The chief advantages were:

1. They possess, under many conditions of terrain and weather, a wider range of strategic and tactical speeds than do any other ground troops.
2. They possess, again under suitable conditions, more rapid tactical mobility than do any other ground troops.
3. Their armor gives them such immunity to many present types of small-arms fire that they can develop a maximum of tactical effect in a minimum of time.[48]

The chief disadvantages were:

1. Being blind, deaf, and having no sensory nerves nor instinct of self-preservation, they are very fatiguing to operate.
2. At night, in the presence of the enemy, they are practically incapable of independent movement.
3. They are extremely sensitive to ground and weather conditions.[49]

Patton believed the result of these advantages and disadvantages was that mechanized forces were most useful only for certain missions. Reconnaissance and counter-reconnaissance were the most important roles for armored cars because in these roles they used their speed and maneuverability to deploy in advance of the main force. Patton also envisioned the creation of vehicles, remarkably similar to more modern armored personnel carriers, to transport infantrymen alongside the armored cars.[50] As far as tanks were concerned, he believed that they were most successful against prepared defenses. Tanks were still too slow and mechanically unreliable to be used in long-range operations. Patton ended his speech by urging caution when dealing with any motorized and mechanized vehicles because they could never be produced in sufficient numbers to make up a large portion of any nation's army. This public lecture again demonstrated Patton's unwillingness to support both sides in the debate over mechanization.

In 1940, after the formation of the Armored Force, Patton finally decided to abandon horse cavalry and return to tanks. This choice again reflected his careerism. Just as Patton's earlier return to cavalry promoted his advancement, now his transfer to the Armored Force did the same thing. As a result of his being an umpire at the Third Army Maneuvers in Louisiana, Patton clearly knew that horse cavalry was on the decline. The question was how to transfer to the Armored Force, since he had been so willing to abandon tanks after World War I. He wrote to Major General Adna R. Chaffee, Jr., the chief of the Armored Force,

The 3rd Cavalry Regiment trooper drilling at Fort Myer, Virginia. (*USCM*)

to plead his case but was restricted by traditions of the service from explicitly stating what he desired.[51] Chaffee was able to divine Patton's real meaning, because two weeks later, Chaffee replied:

> I put you on my preferred list as a brigade commander for an armored brigade. I think it is a job which you could do to the queen's taste, and I need just such a man of your experience in command of an armored brigade. With two light armored regiments and a regiment of tanks employed in a mobile way, I think you could go to town. We have an enormous job in front of us to get this thing organized, trained and going in a minimum of time.... I shall always be happy to know that you are around close in any capacity when there is fighting to be done.[52]

Patton arrived at Fort Benning, Georgia, on July 27, 1940, and assumed command of the 2nd Armored Brigade, 2nd Armored Division. His decision to transfer paid off quickly. Only two months after reporting to Fort Benning, Patton was promoted to brigadier general and appointed the commander of the 2nd Armored Division. Within only a few months, therefore, Patton rose from a colonel and regimental commander in the horse cavalry to a brigadier general and divisional commander in the Armored Force.

In early September 1940, before Patton received his promotion and division command, he received a letter from the Chief of Cavalry, Major General John K. Herr. In this letter, Herr offered to give Patton command of the 1st Cavalry Division. Herr's offer provided Patton two separate opportunities. First, he could return to his first love—horse cavalry. Second, a promotion to brigadier

Fencing squad, 3rd Cavalry Regiment at Fort Myer, Virginia. (*USCM*)

general would be forthcoming with the division command. Despite these obvious temptations, Patton rejected the offer:

> I have kept this letter for a long time trying to make up my mind about your generous and flattering thoughts about me and the Cavalry Div. Of course it is the dream of every cavalry man who is worth a damn to command that outfit and I think I could do a job of it. However I have decided that as I was selected to come here to help make this Brigade I should in loyalty finish that job. You are probably the only person who can realise [*sic.*] how hard it was for me to write the above—I think in my case you would have done the same thing.[53]

Patton then proceeded to discuss the Armored Force, which he believed was "pure cavalry in their functions and tactics."[54] Patton had made his final break with horse cavalry.

While Patton had abandoned any chance of going back to the cavalry, he had not abandoned the concept of horse cavalry. In a letter to a friend, he confessed that, "In spite of my gasoline affiliations, I am convinced that the day of the horse is far from over and that under many circumstances horse cavalry and horse-drawn artillery are more important than ever."[55] When, in the spring of 1941, the Cavalry Board asked him to comment on whether to retain the saber as an issue weapon, Patton responded at length and in the affirmative: "A cold steel weapon is not only desirable but vitally necessary."[56] The infantry still used the bayonet, though few people were ever killed with it. Patton reasoned that the cavalry saber should be retained for the same purpose—in order to intimidate the enemy.

By the end of World War II, the battlefield dominance of mechanized forces—and Patton's own swift advancement in mechanized leadership—prompted him to commit more firmly to an agenda of mechanization.[57] During the war, Patton was too preoccupied with combat to pay much attention to the question of horses. Soon after the war, however, Herr wrote Patton to ask whether the Army needed to retain horse cavalry and how useful a corps of horse cavalry would have been during the war. Patton replied that he indeed believed that the Army needed to retain one horse cavalry division for use under specific and difficult circumstances. As for the idea of a corps of horse cavalry, he believed that, in almost all of the campaigns in Northern Europe and the Mediterranean, horses were of little use and might actually have hampered American forces.[58] Herr wrote back insisting that horse cavalry could have been of great use during the war, especially in North Africa. He also stated that the Soviet Union made great use of horse cavalry on the Eastern Front. Patton replied to Herr that, "I don't agree with you one God damn bit."[59] In particular, he believed that Soviet claims regarding their use of horse cavalry were exaggerated, "particularly since I have seen units that they call cavalry."[60]

The majority of cavalry officers stayed relatively neutral, or at least silent, in the debate over mechanization and were ultimately "pragmatic" enough to delay their decisions until technology and military theory had reached a point of agreement. The same could not be said of Patton. During the entire period from the beginning of World War I to the end of World War II, Patton continually supported both sides in the debate over mechanization. After having served with the Tank Corps during World War I, he still reaffirmed the necessity of horse cavalry. Then, during the interwar period, when he had returned to horse cavalry, Patton refused to dismiss the usefulness of mechanized forces. Finally, following World War II, he stated that the Army needed an entire horse cavalry division on active duty for possible use in future conflicts. While Patton's ambivalence may well have reflected uncertainly over the technological maturity of mechanization, it is clear that each of his oscillations proved beneficial to his career ambitions and mark him as an important and perhaps only "Compromiser" on this issue.

Private Hall, Troop A, 3rd Cavalry Regiment, on duty at the guard house, Fort Brown, Brownsville, Texas, 1915. (*USCM*)

7

U.S. Cavalry in World War II and the Post-War U.S. Army

Despite the U.S. Army Chief of Staff's decision to create the separate Armored Force, cavalry remained a combat arm of the U.S. Army until 1950. With the loss of the 7th Cavalry Brigade (which became the basis for the 1st Armored Division), the cavalry branch struggled to find a viable place on the modern battlefield. The branch's problems were compounded when many cavalry officers requested transfers to the Armored Force. These men recognized that the Army's new arm of mobility was the Armored Force and that horse cavalry was no longer viable on the modern battlefield. From this large pool of applicants, the chief of the Armored Force, Major General Adna R. Chaffee, Jr., was able to pick the cream of the crop. Men such as Patton, Lucian Truscott, Ernie Harmon, Willis Crittenberger, I. D. White, and Willard Holbrooke, Jr., were soon members of the Armored Force and it was dominated by cavalrymen during World War II.

As National Guard and Reserve cavalry regiments were called to active federal service from 1940 onwards, they found that the senior leadership of the Army had abandoned the idea of horse cavalry. The Reserve cavalry regiments were then disbanded and their assets used to form Tank Destroyer and Signal Aircraft Warning battalions, while the Regular Army and National Guard cavalry regiments served in one of three forms: as dismounted (infantry) regiments in the China–Burma–India or Pacific Theaters, or as either armored battalions or mechanized reconnaissance groups in Europe.[1]

Only one horse cavalry unit of the U.S. Army saw combat during World War II. The 26th Cavalry Regiment (Philippine Scouts), which was composed of American officers and Filipino NCOs and enlisted men, fought horse-mounted against the Japanese during the Philippine Campaign of 1941–42. The 26th Cavalry, stationed at Fort Stotsenburg and under the command of Colonel Clinton A. Pierce, was organized with two squadrons of three troops each and had a strength of only fifty-four officers and 784 enlisted men.[2] During the Philippine Campaign, the 26th Cavalry, which owing to its American officers and long-service troopers was considered far more professional than most units

Troops of the 10th Cavalry Regiment present arms while in bivouac on May 28, 1941. (*ISCARL*)

of the Philippine Army, was frequently called upon to stop Japanese attacks when Filipino units retreated without orders. After only two weeks of combat (December 10–December 24, 1941), the 26th Cavalry was already reduced to 450 officers and men.[3] Their efforts were not in vain though, as Major General Jonathan Wainwright, commander of Philippine Division and then U.S. Army Forces Far East during the Philippine Campaign, said of the regiment: "Here was true cavalry delaying action, fit to make a man's heart sing. Pierce ... upheld the best traditions of the cavalry service."[4] On January 24, 1942, Pierce's excellent command of the 26th Cavalry was rewarded when he was given command of the Western Sector during the defense of the Bataan Peninsula and promoted to brigadier general on January 30.[5]

After forage ran out for their horses and mules on March 15, the 26th Cavalry was forced to slaughter the animals to help feed the starving soldiers on Bataan. The regiment, now under the command of Colonel Lee C. Vance, continued to fight on foot and was often called up to stiffen various points in the I Philippine Corps' line. The 26th Cavalry, along with the 45th Infantry Regiment (Philippine Scouts), was designated the corps reserve, because both of these regiments were considered to be more reliable than the units of the Philippine Army.[6] Again and again, the troopers of the 26th Cavalry were called upon halt Japanese advances until, by April 8, the total strength of the regiment amounted to only 300 officers and men.[7] The regiment finally surrendered with the rest of the I Philippine Corps on April 9, 1942.[8]

Jonathan M. Wainwright, commanding officer of Fort Myer, being promoted to the rank of brigadier general on November 11, 1938. Sergeant Major Timothy Carragher (left), of the 16th Field Artillery Regiment, and Sergeant Major Frank Benegas, of the 3rd Cavalry Regiment, the highest ranking non-commissioned officers of the post, were chosen to make the presentation. (*LOC*)

Officers of the 26th Cavalry Regiment (Philippine Scouts), *c.* 1936. (*USCM*)

Several irregular horse cavalry and other mounted units (many using mules) were formed during World War II, though these were almost exclusively used in the Italian and China–Burma–India theaters, where the terrain made motor transport difficult or impossible.[9] However, the last formally organized horse cavalry unit in the Army, after the 26th Cavalry Regiment's surrender, was the U.S. Military Academy Cavalry Squadron (Colored) stationed at West Point, New York, which had white officers and African American NCOs and enlisted men. The job of the squadron was to train cadets in horsemanship.[10]

While horse cavalry scarcely existed in the U.S. Army during World War II, many units carrying the cavalry name and history continued to distinguish themselves. For instance, each infantry division (excluding airborne divisions) included a mechanized cavalry troop to provide reconnaissance, while each armored division included either a mechanized cavalry squadron or an armored reconnaissance battalion for the same purpose. While these armored division reconnaissance units had different designations, in practice they were organized almost identically and, in fact, several changed their designation during the war. In addition, mechanized cavalry groups were organized to provide corps-level reconnaissance. These mechanized cavalry groups were organized from the personnel of fourteen remaining regular Army or and National Guard horse cavalry regiments.[11]

U.S. Army Command and General Staff School Colored Detachment, *c.* 1928. The detachment, which was created on June 15, 1909, and disestablished on October 12, 1931, later became part of the 10th Cavalry Regiment. (*ISCARL*)

Staged photo of an M3 tank crew inexplicably dismounting to use small arms, Fort Knox, Kentucky, June 1942. (*LOC*)

Cavalrymen from the Weapons Troop, 4th Brigade, 2nd Cavalry Division preparing to fire an 81-mm mortar at Camp Funston, Kansas, during World War II.
Left to right: Pvt. R.A. Greene, ammunition carrier; Pfc. J.E. Williams, first gunner; and Cpl. C.T. Babb, observer. (*ISCARL*)

Infantryman next to a halftrack at Fort Knox, Kentucky, June 1942. (*LOC*)

Other than the 26th Cavalry Regiment, only two cavalry regiments fought as non-divisional elements. These regiments, the 112th Cavalry and the 124th Cavalry, were both part of the 56th Cavalry Brigade (Texas National Guard) prior to the outbreak of war.[12] During the war, the 112th Cavalry was dismounted and served in the Southwest Pacific Theater, participating in the New Guinea, Bismarck Archipelago, Leyte, and Luzon Campaigns. Following the war, the regiment was part of the occupation force in Japan until it was inactivated in 1946.[13] The 124th Cavalry was also dismounted and served in the China–Burma–India Theater as part of the MARS Task Force.[14] The regiment, which fought some 300 miles behind Japanese lines and relied on airdrop for supplies, participated in the Central Burma and India–Burma Campaigns.[15]

In Europe, where almost all mechanized cavalry units fought, a post-war study, General Board Report No. 49, "Tactics, Employment, Technique, Organization, and Equipment of Mechanized Cavalry Units," examined the actual missions assigned to mechanized cavalry units. Mechanized cavalry units engaged in "defensive combat, including defense, delaying action, and holding of key terrain until the arrival of main forces" in 33 percent of their missions, "special operations, including acting as a mobile reserve, providing for security and control of rear areas, and operating as an army information service" in 29 percent of their missions, "security for other arms, including blocking, screening, protecting flanks, maintaining contact between larger units, and filling gaps" in 25 percent of their missions, "offensive combat, including attack, pursuit, and exploitation" in 10 percent of their missions, and actual reconnaissance in only 3 percent of their missions.[16] Thus, reconnaissance, which most non-cavalry officers regarded as the only remaining function of cavalry on the modern battlefield even in its newly mechanized state, was seldom actually performed.

The General Board Report also found that mechanized cavalry units fought dismounted twice as often as they fought mounted.[17] While dismounted combat was a common practice for the cavalry since the Civil War, it was not the intended combat method for mechanized cavalry and these troops were neither trained nor equipped for that role. After the war, a group of senior mechanized cavalrymen concluded the missions assigned to mechanized cavalry, especially "reconnaissance with minimum of fighting," were unsound and that their proper mission "should be combat."[18] They believed "the future role of mechanized-cavalry should be the traditional cavalry role of a highly mobile, heavily armed and lighted equipped combat force, and that the capability of mechanized cavalry, particularly that normally operating under the corps, to perform that role, should be exploited."[19]

While divisional cavalry troops and squadrons and corps cavalry groups were similarly equipped and organized, the General Board Report found they were employed in different ways. For instance, cavalry groups engaged in offensive and defensive operations significantly more often (43 percent of operations) than divisional cavalry (15 percent of operations).[20] In addition, divisional cavalry performed reconnaissance missions more often (13 percent of operations) than cavalry groups (3 percent of operations).[21]

Detachment of African American cavalry troops stationed at Ft. Myer, Virginia, are shown participating in the Memorial Day Parade, Washington, D.C., 1942. (*ISCARL*)

In April 1942, a cavalry unit charging during a training exercise at Fort Riley, Kansas. (*LOC*)

Color Guard of the 9th Cavalry Regiment heads for the parade grounds to take part in a regimental review during World War II. (*ISCARL*)

Since the cavalry group had no specific written doctrine, and was employed in such a wide variety of missions, its officers and troopers improvised. While these individuals performed well under difficult circumstances, there were obvious weaknesses in the organization of the cavalry group. These weaknesses generally revolved around the group's small size. Since the group only had a headquarters and headquarters troop (HHT) and two combat squadrons, it was improperly organized to execute the traditional combat doctrine of two-thirds of a unit's combat power in action, while one-third of a unit's combat power was in reserve. This deficiency resulted in the commander being forced to either leave too much (an entire squadron or half his combat power) or too little (one or two troops) in reserve. Ironically, the two squadron organization was based exclusively on peacetime manpower restrictions. Likewise, the cavalry group lacked any organic combat support or service support assets, which resulted in poor coordination when such units were attached.[22] The Army would have solved most of these problems had it used the wartime structure of a cavalry regiment—three combat squadrons. With three squadrons in addition to the HHT, the wartime cavalry regiment possessed enough combat power (and a proper organization) to perform its missions.[23]

The cavalry squadron, in contrast to the group, was better organized. The organization of the cavalry squadron included an HHT, three reconnaissance troops, a light tank company, and a mechanized assault gun company.[24, 25] The large number and diversity of units allowed the cavalry squadron to more effectively deal with different tactical situations.[26] The divisional cavalry reconnaissance troop, while well organized, was severely hampered by a lack of heavy caliber firepower. The troop's primary weapons, which included the 37-mm gun, .30- and .50-caliber machine guns, and the 60-mm mortar, were effective against infantry in the open, but relatively useless against entrenched infantry or heavier formations.[27] When the troop was forced to dismount and engage entrenched infantry, the cavalrymen forfeited their tactical mobility and lacked the small arms firepower of an infantry company—particularly in that mechanized cavalrymen were usually armed with carbines and submachine guns, rather than rifles, due to the cramped space in their vehicles.

The primary vehicles used by mechanized cavalry units were Jeeps, armored cars, light tanks, and mechanized assault guns.[28, 29] All these vehicles shared several positive traits (including speed, reliability, and maneuverability), as well as negative traits (little or no armor and a lack of heavy caliber weapons).[30] Both the armored car and the ubiquitous Jeep had their defenders and detractors. The effectiveness, or lack thereof, of these vehicles was in direct proportion to the method of their employment. If they were employed with the understanding they were extremely vulnerable to small arms fire, they were effective. If, on the other hand, they were employed with little thought given to their vulnerability, they frequently met with disaster.[31]

Cavalry trooper from a machine gun platoon leading a packhorse over an obstacle during a field problem at Fort Riley, Kansas, in April 1942. (*LOC*)

American troops in an armored car passing the *Arc de Triomphe* after the liberation of Paris, August 1944. (*NARA*)

The M3/M5 "Stuart" light tank was criticized for both its light armor and small-caliber main gun (37-mm). While most soldiers acknowledged the light armor was a necessary sacrifice for lighter weight and higher speed, they did not understand the decision to mount such a small-caliber main gun.[32] This problem was solved later in the war with the introduction of the M24 "Chaffee" light tank, which mounted a 75-mm low-velocity main gun capable of engaging bunkers and German tanks up to and including the Panzer IV. The M8 mechanized assault gun was an effective weapon which mounted a short-barreled 75-mm main gun. This vehicle helped to make up for the lack of firepower in the rest of the squadron and the only complaint voiced about the M8 was that the troops preferred the 105-mm version of the assault gun then in service with artillery units.[33]

While none of the National Guard or Reserve cavalry divisions were activated during World War II, two of the Regular Army cavalry divisions did see service. The 1st Cavalry Division, organized as a regular army division in 1921, was dismounted in February 1943 prior to being shipped to Australia. Though the 1st Cavalry fought as an infantry division, it retained the old "square" organization of two brigades with two cavalry regiments each, rather than adopting the new "triangular" formation with no brigades and only three regiments. The 1st Cavalry Division, therefore, was larger than an infantry division and included the 5th, 7th, 8th, and 12th Cavalry Regiments.[34] The division spent eight months training in jungle warfare in Australia and New Guinea before it entered combat in the Admiralty Islands in February 1944. After three months of combat, the 1st Cavalry captured all of their objectives and mopped up the remainder of Japanese resistance. Six months of training followed as the division prepared for its participation in the recapture of the Philippines. The 1st Cavalry was one of the main divisions involved in securing the Philippines and remained in those islands until the end of the war.[35] Following the end of World War II, the 1st Cavalry Division was part of the occupation force in Japan until the Korean War. The 2nd Cavalry Division (Colored) did not share the celebrated history of the 1st Cavalry. Arriving in North Africa in March 1944, the 2nd Cavalry and its component units were quickly disbanded and its personnel used to form service and engineer units.[36]

After World War II, the Army was left with the task of policing the American zone of occupied Germany. In order to do so, Major General Ernest N. Harmon, a cavalryman and the wartime commander of the 1st and 2nd Armored Divisions and the XXII Corps, was appointed the commander, in February 1946, of VI Corps, which became the basis for the U.S. Constabulary.[37] The Constabulary, which existed from 1946 to 1952, was a sort of "super-police force" responsible for the entirety of the American zone. The soldiers of the Constabulary were somewhat derisively referred to as the "super-troopers," "lightning police," or the "Circle C Cowboys" (the latter owing to their shoulder insignia of a "C" with a lightning bolt through it). Harmon converted many of the wartime mechanized cavalry groups into constabulary regiments, each with three constabulary squadrons in place of the wartime complement of two mechanized cavalry squadrons. Each

Silhouette of troops from the 124th Cavalry Regiment (Texas National Guard), then part of the 5332nd Brigade (Provisional), a.k.a. Mars Task Force, on the move from Ramgarh Training Center to Myitkyina, Burma, during World War II. (*NARA*)

constabulary squadron had five troops, which were equipped with a combination of light tanks, armored cars, jeeps, motorcycles, and horses.[38] Thus not only did the Constabulary retain the lineage of many of cavalry regiments, but it was also one of the last units to actively use horses.

The organization of the post-war cavalry was an issue of concern within the branch, especially since the Armored Force was a *de facto* separate branch. General Board Report No. 49, "Tactics, Employment, Technique, Organization, and Equipment of Mechanized Cavalry Units" recommended significant changes in the now-mechanized cavalry regiments' organization. The most important of these recommendations was the inclusion of three squadrons, rather than the two included in the wartime cavalry groups, and a squadron organization that included a troop of dragoons, a light tank troop, a troop of 105-mm Howitzers, and three reconnaissance troops.[39, 40] These recommendations were clearly an attempt to correct some of the most glaring failures of the cavalry groups, most particularly their small size and lack of organic infantry support.

In 1948, the Army organized the first post-war cavalry unit—the 3rd Cavalry Regiment—which was organized on a new table of organization and equipment (TO&E). This new TO&E integrated light tank and dragoon formations down to the platoon level. In addition, it included a medium tank troop at the squadron level, rather than the light tank troop recommended by the General Board Report, and replaced the recommended troop of howitzers with a troop of 105-mm assault guns.[41]

In order to properly employ the new cavalry regiments and existing divisional reconnaissance troops, the Army produced new field manuals on the use of cavalry. These manuals made it clear mechanized cavalry's doctrine was identical to horse cavalry's—offensive and defensive combat, both mounted and dismounted.[42] "For successful accomplishment of these missions, [they were] ... organized, equipped, and trained to attack, defend, or to delay."[43] The Army, therefore, acknowledged that cavalry was a set of missions, rather than a mode of transportation to the battlefield.

Captain James E. Stokes, *c.* 1939. (*USCM*)

Since the Armored Force was not a permanent branch within the Army, many cavalrymen continued to serve in tank units while still technically remaining in the cavalry branch. Beginning in 1947, it appeared that rather than make the Armored Force a permanent branch, the Army might instead merge Armored Force officers into the cavalry to begin referring to the branch as the Armored Cavalry. This idea survived until the U.S. Congress passed the Army Organization Act of 1950, which established the Armor branch and stated that it was "a continuation of the cavalry."[44] This act, therefore, meant the end of the cavalry as an Army branch. Though many units retained their cavalry designation and "air cavalry" became synonymous with the Vietnam War, the cavalry branch, which had been created during the American Revolution and served with distinction over the next 150 years, had ceased to exist.

Conclusion

During the interwar period, three groups and an individual cavalry officer pursued different rationales in dealing with mechanization and horse cavalry. The "traditionalists" believed that the horse was a necessary component of the branch, lending the cavalry its identity. The "modernizers" argued that mechanized vehicles enhanced or even revived cavalry's traditional function, since mechanized vehicles amplified what "modernizers" considered the cavalry's defining characteristic—mobility. The "pragmatists" were willing to define the cavalry in terms of whichever side dominated. The "compromiser" George S. Patton, Jr., attempted to accommodate both the horse and the mechanized vehicle within the cavalry. The eventual fate of the U.S. Cavalry was decided by the interplay between the "traditionalists" and the "modernizers."

During the 1920s, the lack of technological development meant that few cavalry officers, including some of those who later numbered among the "modernizers," seriously thought that mechanized vehicles could supplant the horse, or even become a major force, on the future battlefield. Therefore, the "traditionalists" dominated the decade, and most cavalry officers identified themselves as supporters of the horse. The "traditionalists" interpreted World War I as a historical aberration caused by the presence of large armies within a small geographic space with excellent road and rail networks immediately behind the front lines. These conditions allowed for the creation of immobile trench-lines and mass slaughter. The "traditionalists" believed that, in warfare fought anywhere else in the world, these conditions could not be recreated and, therefore, the horse continued to play a dominant role on all other battlefields. At the same time, since the circumstances of World War I were impossible to recreate anywhere else, mechanized vehicles had little or no use in any other type of future conflict and were nothing more than a curiosity. During this decade, most cavalry officers tended to agree that mechanized vehicles were used successfully only under extremely limited circumstances, which allowed the "traditionalists" to direct the Army's meager funding almost exclusively toward horse cavalry.

Private Price, Troop A, 3rd Cavalry Regiment, *c*. 1916. (*USCM*)

During the 1930s, however, technological improvements led many cavalry officers, including some former supporters of the horse, to reexamine mechanized vehicles. During this decade, the ranks of the "modernizers" began to increase and, though they acknowledged that the horse still had a role on the modern battlefield, the "modernizers" argued that mechanized vehicles also had a significant place. Therefore, throughout most of this decade, most cavalry officers tended to agree that mechanized vehicles had a sufficient enough role on the battlefield to justify the maintenance of few mechanized cavalry regiments, but most also believed that mechanized vehicles were only an auxiliary to the horse.

During these first two periods of time, the "pragmatists" refused to choose sides in the debate. Most of the "pragmatists" believed that the leaders within the U.S. Army would ultimately make the "right" decision. This faith in the Army's leadership is understandable in an organization that emphasizes loyalty, hierarchy/chain of command, and devotion to duty. While horses remained the dominant "vehicle" of the cavalry, the "pragmatists" did not question their battlefield utility.

Trooper, 3rd Cavalry Regiment, *c*. 1916. (*USCM*)

Toward the end of the 1930s, as international and technological developments made mechanized vehicles more prominent in military theory and on the battlefield, the positions of the groups within the cavalry evolved. The "modernizers" became openly and loudly vocal in their support for an expanded role of mechanized vehicles in the cavalry. The "pragmatists" began to realize that the "modernizers" were correct about the influence of mechanized vehicles in the approaching war, though they remained largely silent until 1940. The "traditionalists," however, refused to acknowledge that anything had changed and continued to insist that the horse remained a dominant military "vehicle." The German invasion of Poland in September 1939 and the Louisiana Maneuvers in May 1940 proved to be the final acts in this drama for all concerned. The decision to create the separate Armored Force allowed the "modernizers" to control the course of mechanization, but it also signaled the end of horse cavalry to the "pragmatists," most of whom then abandoned the cavalry branch. By the end of the 1930s, therefore, the vast majority of cavalry officers, both "modernizers" and the "pragmatists," agreed that mechanized vehicles had a dominant role on the battlefield and that the horse only existed as a minor auxiliary. However, the "traditionalists" refused to acknowledge the logic of the horse's now subordinate role. As a result, the "traditionalists" spent World War II either relegated to desk assignments or in retirement because they refused to serve with the Armored Force or mechanized cavalry formations. The "compromiser," Patton, followed the general trend of being more pro-horse in the 1920s, more pro-mechanization in the 1930s, and made his final break with the cavalry branch following the Louisiana Maneuvers in 1940.

As the "traditionalists" feared, the U.S. Army from World War II onward has been radically different—technologically, socially, and culturally—from the pre-World War II Army. The career of an Army cavalry officer after America's entry into World War II was distinct from that of cavalryman who served until that point. The enormous and rapid growth of the Army meant that instead of officers being almost exclusively the product of West Point or other military academies, a great many officers served previously in the National Guard or Reserves, were commissioned from the ranks, or were the product of Officer Candidate Schools (OCS) or the Reserve Officers Training Course (ROTC). The Army, then, had inculcated these new officers with few, if any, of the traditional military officers' culture. Their educational backgrounds were also very diverse, from graduate education at major American universities to high school diplomas.

These new officers served not in a close-knit, almost family-like, environment, which existed prior to World War II, but rather in an enormous Army bureaucracy. At its peak, the Army numbered 8 million men and women, which meant that it was impossible for them to know anyone other than the members of their individual units. Since they were not from military families, their historical memory of the Army was limited to their own time in service and, possibly, to their fathers' service during World War I. While, the enormity of World War II did in some ways resemble their fathers' service in World War I, the conflicts themselves were so different in nature that there seemed to be little or no historical continuity between the conflicts.

The equipment and training of these officers were also markedly different from that of earlier periods. Among their equipment, a semi-automatic rifle (M1 Garand) had replaced the bolt-action rifles of earlier periods and gave the American soldier a decided advantage in firepower. The machine gun had become one of the dominant battlefield weapons, and animal "horse-power" now gave way to mechanical "horse-power" as trucks and tanks came into their own. In the realm of training, senior officers in the Army took professional military education very seriously and even many of the "temporary" officers attended an abbreviated version of the Command and General Staff School.

The life of a cavalry officer in the period after the outbreak of World War II, then, changed a great deal from that of a cavalry officer in the preceding period. World War II did not serve merely as a significant break in the historical continuity of the cavalry. Rather, it represented a distinct break in terms of traditions and practices of the cavalry. Rather than playing a minor role, technology changed warfare forever—from airpower to mechanization to the atomic bomb.

While acknowledging the importance of technology, the human element was crucial to the path of technological development. Defining the social differences between the groups of cavalry officers might be useful for the purposes of this work. Unfortunately, the similar backgrounds of these officers make their differing opinions

Halftrack scout cars manufactured by the White Motor Company in Cleveland, Ohio, December 1941. (*LOC*)

on the subject of mechanization that much more resistant to tidy explanations. The categories of "traditionalist," "modernizer," "pragmatist," or "compromiser" do not neatly correspond to observable social, cultural, economic, or regional groups. For instance, the trinity of modern social history—race, gender, and class—can be eliminated immediately as determinants of opinion, because these officers were all white males of middle- to upper-class backgrounds. Many historians might argue that the graduates of the United States Military Academy (the curriculum of which changed so little from the nineteenth century) were more "traditional" in their thinking on the topic of mechanization. However, graduates of West Point can be found among "modernizers," "pragmatists," and the "compromiser," as well as "traditionalists." Perhaps the familial relations of the tiny interwar officer corps—a group that often married within its own network of families—played a role. Again, unfortunately, this idea should be discounted because Chaffee, perhaps the most important "modernizer," was from an even more prominent military family than Herr, who was perhaps the most important "traditionalist." Regionalism might be a cause, but, again, it does not appear to be a factor, because no particular region was dominant among any of the identified groups. The age of the men in question was also not a factor. Van Voorhis, a "modernizer," started his military career during the Spanish-American War, but so had Hawkins, who was a "traditionalist." The career paths of the officers in question were also very similar. Almost all of these officers attended the Command and General Staff School or one of its predecessors as well as served in staff, education, and command positions throughout their careers. Likewise, almost all of these officers served in France during World War I.

In short, these officers had relatively similar life experiences, which complicates the task of explaining their sharp differences of opinion. Perhaps for Chaffee and Herr, the battlefield conditions of World War I meant different things. In theory, Chaffee may have viewed the World War I battlefield conditions as emblematic of the end of an old way of warfare and the beginning of a new way, while for Herr, perhaps those exact same battlefield conditions were merely a historical aberration never to reappear.

During the interwar period, the Army's long-term technological direction was particularly unclear due to the absence of a defined foreign or domestic threat to the contiguous forty-eight states. During the nineteenth century, the potential foreign threat of either the United Kingdom with its dominion in Canada or that of Mexico to the south shaped United States' military strategy. Also during that century, the continuous danger of conflict with North American Indians posed a possible domestic threat. Lastly, around the turn of the twentieth century, imperialism created situations in which America defended or pacified its colonial possessions. By 1920, however, no obvious foreign threat existed from the U.S. Army's perspective[1] and both the North American Indians and the inhabitants of our colonial possessions were completely pacified.

During the 1920s, the lack of a major threat to the United States justified the neglect of the military in the minds of the American public. After the stock market crash in 1929, even less attention was paid to national defense, as pressing domestic

Above: The tallest and shortest members of the troop, 2nd Cavalry Regiment, *c*. 1936. (*USCM*)

Opposite: Cavalry trooper Billie Rondue of the 2nd Cavalry Regiment during World War I. (*USCM*)

Billie

issues claimed the focus of the American government and people. Although foreign powers renewed their threats to the United States during the 1930s, difficult economic times appeared to justify the continued neglect of the military.

The lack of economic resources contributed to mechanization's state of limbo throughout the interwar period. Between 1921 and 1939, the average yearly strength of the Army was only 126,126, while the average yearly budget appropriated by the Congress was only $318 million.[2] The low point for the Army, in terms of manpower, came in 1923, when the total strength was only 111,341. In 1939, the high point in manpower terms, the total strength was 167,712.[3] The low point for the Army's budget occurred in 1935, when the Congress appropriated a total of only $250 million. In 1939, the high point in budgetary terms, the Congress approved $449 million.[4] The manpower and budgetary increases that took place by 1939 were mostly a reaction to the increasingly volatile world situation. By 1939, Japan had invaded China, Italy had invaded and conquered Ethiopia, and Germany had consumed both Austria and Czechoslovakia without firing a shot. Nevertheless, on September 1, 1939, when Germany invaded Poland, the U.S. Army still ranked as only the seventeenth largest army in the world, behind smaller and less industrialized nations such as Sweden, Yugoslavia, and Turkey.[5]

The results of mechanization were ultimately so radical that no one could have predicted how much they would change the U.S. Army by the end of World War II. Though a few iconoclastic military thinkers[6] envisioned a completely mechanized army of the future, the vast majority of military officers throughout the world believed that mechanization was merely an adjunct to the existing military organization. In addition, mechanization did not take exactly the route that even the most radical military theorists believed. As with many other technological shifts throughout human history, the end results were different than the perceived path of development. The effects of the stirrup, gunpowder, and machine gun are a few military examples, but this analogy may be extended to non-military developments as well, such as railroads, automobiles, and computers.

The debate over mechanization went through three distinct phases. During the first phase (approximately from 1920 to 1928), most cavalry officers believed that it was technologically impossible to mechanize the cavalry completely. Tanks were lumbering 5-mph vehicles that broke down frequently and guzzled gasoline. Therefore, the existing mechanized vehicles were physically incapable of performing traditional cavalry missions. Under these circumstances, there was little enthusiasm for mechanization within the cavalry except from a small core group of officers who served in the Tank Corps during World War I.

During the second phase (approximately from 1928 to 1938), the common perception among cavalry officers was that it was financially/industrially impossible to mechanize the cavalry completely. The development of radical new designs, specifically those produced by inventor J. Walter Christie, demonstrated that mechanized vehicles were theoretically capable of performing cavalry missions. Under the circumstances, cavalry officers then examined the state of the tiny and chronically underfunded U.S. Army. During the next war, they concluded, the Army would have some mechanized vehicles, but that the excessive cost of these vehicles, coupled with the equipment shortfalls they experienced during World War I, meant that only a small number of mechanized units would be formed.[7] These mechanized units, therefore, were nothing more than an auxiliary (important, but, necessarily small) to horse cavalry.

During the third and final phase (approximately from 1938 to 1942), as a result of the enormous growth of manufacturing in both America (as much, if not more during this period, to supply the British Commonwealth as to supply the U.S. military) and Europe, most cavalry officers believed that it was now both technologically and financially/industrially possible to mechanize the cavalry completely. By this point, only the most "traditional" cavalry officers refused to accept the obvious and existing situation—that mechanized vehicles, rather than horses, were already dominating warfare. The "pragmatist" and "compromiser" cavalry officers finally joined the "modernizers" in their support of mechanization and abandoned the horse cavalry to serve with the Armored Force after its formation in 1940, which confirmed their new allegiance.

The seven cavalry officers examined in this work were divided between "traditionalists," "modernizers," "pragmatists," and the "compromiser." The "traditionalists," John K. Herr and Hamilton S. Hawkins, supported the horse and were opposed to mechanization and ultimately demonstrated that their support and opposition were based on nothing more than traditionalism in both sentiment and culture. The "modernizers," Adna R. Chaffee, Jr., Guy V. Henry, Jr., Leon B. Kromer, and Daniel Van Voorhis, supported mechanization and attempted to adjust the cavalry's self-concept to accommodate both the incoming and outgoing technology. The "pragmatists," while difficult to document because of their indifference or practicality, appear to have taken a "wait and see" attitude toward the future of mechanization. During the interwar struggle between the "traditionalists" and "modernizers," the "pragmatists" were more often than not simply spectators. Lastly, Patton offered vocal support for the maintenance of both horse and mechanized formations, which marked him as a "compromiser" who envisioned a possible future involving both forms of cavalry.

In 1935, Lieutenant Colonel Jonathan M. Wainwright, the Assistant Commandant of the Cavalry School, stated that "The Cavalry School is accused by the strong proponents of the horse of being too mechanical minded, and, by the stout supporters of mechanization, of being over 'horsey.' Both arraignments are absurd."[8] In general, Wainwright's assertion concerning the Cavalry School is a fitting epitaph for the U.S. Cavalry as a whole. During the interwar period, while "modernizers" and "traditionalists" argued for or against mechanization, the "pragmatists" were willing to hold off judgment until they were certain whether technological improvements eliminated the mechanical shortcomings of early mechanized vehicles and Patton attempted a "compromise" wherein both horses and mechanized vehicles had a role in future warfare. This internal conflict influenced the organization of the U.S. Army during World War II—the cavalry branch, in Jeeps and armored cars, was restricted to reconnaissance and counter-reconnaissance, while the Armored Force was the principal maneuver arm on the battlefield.

Officer of the 2nd Cavalry Regiment, *c.* 1916. (*USCM*)

Endnotes

Introduction

1. Coffman, *Old Army: A Portrait of the American Army in Peacetime, 1784–1898* (1986).
2. Nenninger, *Leavenworth Schools and the Old Army: Education, Professionalism, and the Officer Corps of the United States Army, 1881–1918* (1978).
3. Linn, *Guardians of Empire: The U.S. Army and the Pacific, 1902–1940* (1997); and Weigley, *History of the United States Army* (1984).

Chapter 1

1. Stubbs and Connor, *Armor-Cavalry*, Part I: *Regular Army and Army Reserve* (1969), pp. 33–35.
2. Tompkins, *Chasing Villa: The Last Campaign of the U.S. Cavalry* (1934), pp. 72–73.
3. Eisenhower, *Intervention!: The United States and the Mexican Revolution, 1913–1917* (1993), pp. 248–49.
4. Clendenen, *Blood On The Border: The United States Army And The Mexican Irregulars* (1969), pp. 238–239.
5. Benjamin D. Foulois; Report of Operations, 1st Aero Squadron, Mexican Punitive Expedition, 15 March 1916–15 August 1916; Adjutant General's Office, Record Group 407; National Archives and Records Administration, College Park, Maryland.
6. Charles S. Farnsworth; Report of Operations, Base of Communications, Mexican Punitive Expedition, 19 June 1916–5 February 1917; Adjutant General's Office, Record Group 407; National Archives and Records Administration, College Park, Maryland.
7. *Ibid.*
8. Foulois eventually became a major general and chief of the U.S. Army Air Corps from 1931 to 1935.
9. *Ibid.*, pp. 1–2.
10. Francis H. Pope; Report of Motor Transport Operations, Mexican Punitive Expedition, 16 March 1916–5 February 1917; Adjutant General's Office, Record Group 407; National Archives and Records Administration, College Park, Maryland.
11. Meriwether L. Walker; Report of Engineer Operations, Mexican Punitive Expedition, 1 July 1916–5 February 1917; Adjutant General's Office, Record Group 407; National Archives and Records Administration, College Park, Maryland.
12. Pope, p. 1.

13. See: Blackburn, *United States Army and the Motor Truck: A Case Study in Standardization* (1996).
14. James Parker, 'First Endorsement On "A Report On A Two Hundred Mile Experimental Cavalry March"', *Cavalry Journal* 27 (January 1917): pp. 363–364.
15. Robert Michie; Memorandum to the Chief of Staff, May 14, 1917; Exclusion Of Cavalry Organizations From The Call For Federal Service; Records of the War Department General and Special Staffs, RG 165; National Archives and Records Administration, College Park, Maryland.
16. For information on the Eastern Front during World War I, see: Stone, *Eastern Front, 1914–1917* (1975). For information on the effects of World War I and the Russo-Polish War on military thinking in Eastern Europe, see: Zaloga and Madej, *Polish Campaign, 1939* (1985); and Turner, *Genesis of the Soviet 'Deep Operation': The Stalin-Era Doctrine for Large-Scale Offensive Maneuver Warfare* (1988).
17. Office of the Chief of Staff; Memorandum for the Adjutant General of the Army, Raising of Additional Cavalry Regiments, 13 March 1918; Office of the Chief of Staff, Record Group 194; National Archives and Records Administration, College Park, Maryland.
18. John Biddle, Acting Chief of Staff; Organization of a Cavalry Division (Regular); 15th Cavalry Division, Organization; Office of the Chief of Staff, Record Group 194; National Archives and Records Administration, College Park, Maryland.
19. C. W. Moffett, Historical Branch; Battle Participation, Cavalry Regiments, 2nd Cavalry; Office of the Chief of Staff, Record Group 194; National Archives and Records Administration, College Park, Maryland.
20. Stubbs and Connor, p. 39.
21. Harmon was a major general and commander of the 1st and 2nd Armored Divisions and then the XXI Corps during World War II.
22. Harmon, MacKaye, and MacKaye, *Combat Commander: Autobiography of a Soldier* (1970), pp. 25–6.
23. *Ibid.*, p. 24.
24. *Ibid.*, pp. 26–45.
25. See: Wilson, *Treat 'em Rough!: The Birth of American Armor, 1917–1929* (1989).
26. 'Opinions of Military Leaders on the Value of Cavalry', p. 3; Armistice Day Address at the Kemper Military School, Boonville, Missouri, November 11, 1925; Mexican Border, 1916–1928; Willis D. Crittenberger Papers; U.S. Army Army Heritage & Education Center, Carlisle Barracks, Pennsylvania.
27. *Ibid.*, p. 3.
28. *Ibid.*, p. 1.
29. *Ibid.*, p. 2.
30. *Ibid.*, p. 3.
31. These included, but were not limited to: immature technology, industrial shortfalls, terrain limitations, and supply shortages.

Chapter 2

1. *National Defense Act, Approved June 3, 1913, As Amended by Act Approved June 4, 1920* (1920).
2. Clay, *U.S. Army Order of Battle, 1919–1941*, Volume 2 (2010), pp. 559–653.
3. *Ibid.*, pp. 628–639.
4. *Ibid.*, p. 627.
5. Hofmann, *Through Mobility We Conquer: The Mechanization of U.S. Cavalry* (2006), pp. 78–87.
6. Christie, *Steel Steeds Christie: A Memoir of J. Walter Christie* (1985), pp. 1–2.
7. *Ibid.*, pp. 20–22.

8. *Ibid.*, p. 25.
9. *Ibid.*, p. 27.
10. *Ibid.*, p. 31.
11. C. C. Benson and G. S. Patton, Jr., 'Mechanization and Cavalry', *Cavalry Journal* 39 (April 1930), pp. 237–238.
12. Christie, p. 66.
13. Liddell Hart, *Tanks: The History of the Royal Tank Regiment and Its Predecessors: Heavy Machine-Gun Corps, Tank Corps, and Royal Tank Corps, 1914–1945*, Volume I (1959), pp. 255–63.
14. 'Basic Principles of Experimental Mechanized Force', *Cavalry Journal* 37 (July 1928), pp. 440–441.
15. Adna R. Chaffee, Jr., 'Status of the Mechanized Combat Organization and the Desired Trend in the Future'; Lecture Delivered to the Army War College, Washington, DC, 19 September 1929; Willis D. Crittenberger Papers, U.S. Army Army Heritage & Education Center, Carlisle Barracks, Pennsylvania; and Gillie, *Forging the Thunderbolt: A History of the Development of the Armored Force* (1947), pp. 21–22.
16. Chaffee, 'Status of the Mechanized Combat Organization and the Desired Trend in the Future'; and Gillie, pp. 21–22.
17. Gillie, p. 23.
18. 'Mechanized Force Recommended', *Cavalry Journal* 39 (January 1930), p. 112.
19. *Ibid.*, p. 112.
20. 'Mechanized Force Becomes Cavalry', *Cavalry Journal* 40 (May/June 1931), p. 5.
21. *Ibid.*, p. 6.
22. Gillie, pp. 48–50.
23. Douglas MacArthur, Chief of Staff; 'General Principles to Govern In Extending Mechanization and Motorization Throughout the Army', 1 May 1931; Cavalry Board; Office of the Chief of Cavalry, Record Group 177; National Archives and Records Administration, College Park, Maryland.
24. 'Mechanized Force Becomes Cavalry', *Cavalry Journal* 40 (May/June 1931), p. 6.
25. Gillie, pp. 58–60.
26. *Ibid.*, pp. 52–54.
27. *Ibid.*, pp. 54–56; and R. W. Grow, 'Ten Lean Years: From the Mechanized Force (1930) to the Armored Force (1940)', 7. Robert W. Grow Papers, United States Army Army Heritage & Education Center, Carlisle Barracks, Pennsylvania.
28. Grow, p. 33; and Sawicki, p. 151.
29. 'Cavalry Maneuvers at Fort Riley, Kansas, 1934', *Cavalry Journal* 43 (July/August 1934), p. 5.
30. *Ibid.*, pp. 12–14.
31. Gillie, p. 68.
32. Grow, p. 50.
33. Vehicle Data; 1st Cavalry Regiment (Mechanized), 1 May 1935; Files, 1931–41; Willis D. Crittenberger Papers, U.S. Army Army Heritage & Education Center, Carlisle Barracks, Pennsylvania.
34. B. Palmer, 'Mechanized Cavalry in the Second Army Maneuvers', *Cavalry Journal* 45 (November/December 1936), pp. 461–478.
35. Palmer, pp. 474–477.
36. Gillie, p. 92–93; and Memorandum; 'Data on the Mechanization of a Second Regiment of Cavalry'; Colonel Charles L. Scott to Major General Leon B. Kromer, 8 May 1936; Correspondence, 1921–1942; Office of the Chief of Cavalry, Record Group 177; National Archives and Records Administration, College Park, Maryland.
37. Gillie, pp. 92–93.
38. T. J. Heavey, 'Horse-Mechanized Regiment', *Cavalry Journal* 49 (September/October 1940), p. 424.
39. Stubbs and Connor, p. 70; and Sawicki, p. 114.

40. Clay, *U.S. Army Order of Battle, 1919–1941*, Volume 1 (2010), pp. 219–220, 239–240.
41. A. R. Chaffee, Jr., 'Seventh Cavalry Brigade at the First Army Maneuvers', *Cavalry Journal* 48 (November/December 1939), pp. 450–461.
42. The division included the 1st Cavalry Brigade with the 5th and 12th Cavalry Regiments and the 2nd Cavalry Brigade with the 7th and 8th Cavalry Regiments. Clay, *U.S. Army Order of Battle, 1919–1941*, Volume 2, pp. 596–597.
43. E. E. Schwien, 'Cavalry Division Maneuvers, October, 1939', *Cavalry Journal* 48 (November–December 1939), p. 464.
44. *Ibid.*, p. 464.
45. The Provisional Tank Brigade (66th and 67th Infantry Regiments—Light and Medium Tanks, respectively) had been organized especially for the maneuvers.
46. Gillie, p. 162–163; and Broom, *Commander's Vision In Blue and Grey: The Roles of Adna R. Chaffee, Jr., James H. Wilson, and the American Civil War in the Development of American Armor Doctrine* (1993), p. 216.
47. Gillie, pp. 163–164.
48. *Ibid.*, pp. 166–168; 'Armor' was chosen as the name for the new force in order to avoid using the terms 'Mechanized', previously used by the cavalry, or 'Tank', previously used by the infantry.

Chapter 3

1. Both of these schools were located at Fort Leavenworth, Kansas, and were predecessors of the Command and General Staff College.
2. *Order of Battle of the United States Land Forces in the World War*, Volume 2 (1988), p. 210.
3. He was: the Assistant Commandant of the Cavalry School, Fort Riley, Kansas; the commander of the 3rd Cavalry Regiment, Fort Myer, Virginia; the Chief of Staff of the Philippine Department, Manila; the commander of the 14th Infantry Brigade, Omaha, Nebraska; and the commander of the 1st Cavalry Brigade, Fort Clark, Texas. H. S. Hawkins; Career Highlights. Cullum Number 3586. H. S. Hawkins Papers. Archives of the United States Military Academy, West Point, New York.
4. H. S. Hawkins, 'Cavalry and Mechanized Force', *Cavalry Journal* 40 (September–October 1931), p. 19.
5. *Ibid.*, 'Cavalry and Mechanized Force', p. 19.
6. *Ibid.*, 'Cavalry and Mechanized Force', p. 19.
7. *Ibid.*, 'Cavalry and Mechanized Force', p. 19.
8. *Ibid.*, 'Cavalry and Mechanized Force', p. 20.
9. *Ibid.*, 'Cavalry and Mechanized Force', p. 24.
10. *Ibid.*, 'Cavalry and Mechanized Force', pp. 21–22.
11. H. S. Hawkins; Memorandum; 'Reorganization of Divisions and Higher Units'; 25 November 1935, p. 4; Correspondence, 1921–1942; Office of the Chief of Cavalry, Record Group 177; National Archives and Records Administration, College Park, Maryland.
12. *Ibid.*, p. 4.
13. *Ibid.*, p. 7.
14. H. S. Hawkins, 'We Must Have Cavalry', *Cavalry Journal* 46 (September–October 1937), p. 405.
15. *Ibid.*, p. 406.
16. *Ibid.*, p. 406.
17. *Ibid.*, p. 406.
18. *Ibid.*, p. 407.
19. *Ibid.*, p. 407.
20. *Ibid.*, p. 407.

21. H. S. Hawkins, 'Imagination Gone Wild', *Cavalry Journal* 47 (November–December 1938), p. 491.
22. *Ibid.*, p. 495.
23. *Ibid.*, p. 495.
24. *Ibid.*, p. 497.
25. H. S. Hawkins, 'General Hawkins' Notes', *Cavalry Journal* 49 (May–June 1940), p. 269.
26. *Ibid.*, p. 269.
27. H. S. Hawkins, 'General Hawkins' Notes', *Cavalry Journal* 51 (January–February 1942), p. 48.
28. *Ibid.*, p. 49.
29. H. S. Hawkins, 'General Hawkins' Notes', *Cavalry Journal* 54 (September–October 1945), p. 32.
30. *Order of Battle of the United States Land Forces in the World War*, Volume 2, p. 160.
31. The American Forces in Germany were a small occupation force which remained in Germany until the ratification of a separate peace between Germany and the United States. *Order of Battle of the United States Land Forces in the World War*, Volume 1 (1988), p. 395.
32. He graduated from the Command and General Staff School in 1926 and the Army War College in 1927, then served as an instructor at the Army War College between 1929 and 1931. John K. Herr; Career Highlights. Cullum Number 4112. John K. Herr Papers. Archives of the United States Military Academy, West Point, New York.
33. Memorandum; 'Cavalry Requirements for the United States Army'; John K. Herr to the Adjutant General, p. 3; 5 August 1938; Correspondence 1935–1938; Willis D. Crittenberger Papers; U.S. Army Army Heritage & Education Center, Carlisle Barracks, PA.
34. 'Cavalry Requirements for the United States Army', p. 7.
35. Grow, p. 76.
36. *Ibid.*, p. 76.
37. J. K. Herr, 'What of the Future?', *Cavalry Journal* 48 (January–February 1939), p. 4.
38. See: Piekalkiewicz, *Cavalry in World War II* (1976); and Zaloga and Madej, *Polish Campaign, 1939*.
39. 'Cavalry Affairs Before Congress', *Cavalry Journal* 48 (March–April 1939), p. 130.
40. *Ibid.*, p. 131.
41. *Ibid.*, p. 131.
42. Letter; John K. Herr to Adna R. Chaffee, Jr.; 1 June 1939; Correspondence, 1921–1942; Office of the Chief of Cavalry, Record Group 177; National Archives and Records Administration, College Park, Maryland.
43. *Ibid.*
44. Grow, p. 85.
45. Memorandum; 'Some Observations and Recommendations Pertinent to Any Future Expansion and Development of Mechanized Cavalry Which May Be Contemplated by the War Department'; Adna R. Chaffee, Jr., to the Adjutant General, 15 September 1939; Correspondence, 1921–1942; Office of the Chief of Cavalry, Record Group 177; National Archives and Records Administration, College Park, Maryland.
46. *Ibid.*
47. Daniel Van Voorhis; Endorsement of Memorandum by Adna R. Chaffee, Jr., 18 September 1939; Correspondence, 1921–1942; Office of the Chief of Cavalry, Record Group 177; National Archives and Records Administration, College Park, Maryland.
48. John K. Herr; Endorsement of Memorandum by Adna R. Chaffee, Jr., 9 October 1939; Correspondence, 1921–1942; Office of the Chief of Cavalry, Record Group 177; National Archives and Records Administration, College Park, Maryland.
49. Grow, p. 88.
50. Letter; John K. Herr to George C. Marshall; 3 October 1939. Cullum Number 4112. John K. Herr Papers. Archives of the United States Military Academy, West Point, New York.

51. *Ibid.*
52. Grow, p. 85.
53. Letter; John K. Herr to Frank M. Andrews; 5 January 1940. Cullum Number 4112. John K. Herr Papers. Archives of the United States Military Academy, West Point, New York.
54. *Ibid.*
55. John K. Herr, 'Armored Force', p. 4. Cullum Number 4112. John K. Herr Papers. Archives of the United States Military Academy, West Point, New York.
56. Leon B. Kromer; Lecture on Cavalry; 1 October 1937; Speeches, Articles, Clippings, and Programs; Leon B. Kromer Papers; United States Army Army Heritage & Education Center, Carlisle Barracks, PA.
57. Herr, 'Armored Force', p. 5.
58. *Ibid.*, pp. 5–6.
59. *Ibid.*, pp. 6–7.
60. *Ibid.*, pp. 6–7.
61. Grow, p. 89.
62. Letter; John K. Herr to George C. Marshall; 10 April 1940. Cullum Number 4112. John K. Herr Papers. Archives of the United States Military Academy, West Point, New York.
63. 'Cavalry Affairs in Congress', *Cavalry Journal* 49 (May–June 1940), p. 201.
64. *Ibid.*, p. 204.
65. *Ibid.*, p. 205.
66. *Ibid.*, p. 206.
67. Herr, 'Armored Force', p. 7.
68. *Ibid.*, p. 7.
69. *Ibid.*, p. 8.
70. Memorandum; John K. Herr to Frank M. Andrews; 3 June 1940; Correspondence, 1921–1942; Office of the Chief of Cavalry, Record Group 177; National Archives and Records Administration, College Park, Maryland.
71. *Ibid.*
72. Herr, 'Armored Force', pp. 10–11.
73. During World War II, Armor was not yet a separate branch (which required congressional legislation and did not actually happen until 1950), but rather existed as a 'Force', in order to avoid the legal entanglements.
74. Memorandum; 'Organization of the Armored Force'; Frank M. Andrews to John K. Herr; 19 November 1940. Cullum Number 4112. John K. Herr Papers. Archives of the United States Military Academy, West Point, New York.
75. Memorandum; 'Organization of the Armored Force'; John K. Herr to Frank M. Andrews; 7 December 1940. Cullum Number 4112. John K. Herr Papers. Archives of the United States Military Academy, West Point, New York.
76. Letter; John K. Herr to Innis P. Swift; 13 March 1941; Correspondence, 1921–1942; Office of the Chief of Cavalry, Record Group 177; National Archives and Records Administration, College Park, Maryland.
77. Gabel, *U.S. Army GHQ Maneuvers of 1941* (1991), pp. 118–119.
78. Herr and Wallace, *Story of the U.S. Cavalry, 1775–1942* (1984), p. 250.
79. Gabel, pp. 127–128.
80. Herr, *Story of the U.S. Cavalry*, p. 250.
81. Gabel, p. 171.
82. J. K. Herr, 'Why Should the United States Lag Behind Other Great Powers in the Military Use of Animals?', *Cavalry Journal* 51 (January–February 1942), p. 23.
83. *Ibid.*, p. 23.
84. *Ibid.*, p. 24.
85. *Ibid.*, p. 26.
86. Memorandum; John K. Herr to George C. Marshall; 26 January 1942. Cullum Number 4112. John K. Herr Papers. Archives of the United States Military Academy, West Point, New York.

87. Herr, *Story of the U.S. Cavalry*, p. 252.
88. Letter; Secretary of War Henry L. Stimson to John K. Herr; 11 July 1942. Cullum Number 4112. John K. Herr Papers. Archives of the United States Military Academy, West Point, New York.
89. *Ibid.*
90. *Ibid.*
91. Letter; Lucian K. Truscott, Jr., to John K. Herr; 14 July 1945. Cullum Number 4112. John K. Herr Papers. Archives of the United States Military Academy, West Point, New York.
92. *Ibid.*
93. Letter; Hamilton H. Howze to John K. Herr; 6 May 1946. Cullum Number 4112. John K. Herr Papers. Archives of the United States Military Academy, West Point, New York.
94. *Ibid.*
95. Letter; Ernest N. Harmon to John K. Herr; 25 July 1946. Cullum Number 4112. John K. Herr Papers. Archives of the United States Military Academy, West Point, New York.
96. *Ibid.*
97. Herr, *Story of the U.S. Cavalry*, pp. 253–254.
98. *Ibid.*, pp. 255–256.

Chapter 4

1. Gillie, p. 27.
2. *Ibid.*, p. 28.
3. *Order of Battle of the United States Land Forces in the World War*, Volume 1, pp. 237, 329.
4. Gillie, p. 29.
5. Now, as then, U.S. Army officers rely heavily on the support of their branch to receive the appointments necessary for career advancement. This practice is commonly referred to as "ticket-punching," but it is a well-known fact that officers without certain key assignments find promotion next to impossible.
6. In succession, he was an instructor at the General Staff School (precursor to the Command and General Staff College), Fort Leavenworth, Kansas; the Assistant Chief of Staff for Intelligence (G-2), IV Corps; the G-3, 1st Cavalry Division, Fort Bliss, Texas; a student at the Army War College, Washington, DC; a squadron commander, 3rd Cavalry Regiment, Fort Myer, Virginia; and finally a member of the staff of the Operations and Training Division of the War Department General Staff. Gillie, pp. 28–30, and Broom, pp. 68–9.
7. Gillie, pp. 29–31.
8. Adna R. Chaffee, Jr., 'Status of the Mechanized Combat Organization and the Desired Trend in the Future', p. 2–3; Lecture Delivered to the Army War College, Washington, DC; 19 September 1929; Willis D. Crittenberger Papers, U.S. Army Army Heritage & Education Center, Carlisle Barracks, PA.
9. *Ibid.*, p. 4.
10. *Ibid.*, pp. 4–6.
11. This is not the same Walter C. Short who, while commander of the U.S. Army in Hawaii in 1941, was made infamous by the Pearl Harbor attack. Surprisingly, there were two generals named Walter C. Short in the interwar U.S. Army—one an infantryman and the other a cavalryman.
12. Gillie, pp. 57–58.
13. Nenninger, 'Development of Armor, 1917–1940: A Revised Mechanization Policy', *Armor* 78 (September–October 1969), p. 49.
14. Address by Adna R. Chaffee, Jr., on the Subject of 'Mechanized Cavalry' Before the Army War College, 29 September 1939; Office of the Chief of Cavalry, Record Group 177; National Archives and Records Administration, College Park, Maryland.

15. Grow, p. 84.
16. *Ibid*., p. 86.
17. Following the Spanish-American War, the U.S. Army's regular strength was increased from ten to fifteen cavalry and from twenty-five to thirty infantry regiments.
18. Among other assignments, he served in the Philippines; attended the Army School of the Line, Fort Leavenworth, and the Mounted Service School, Fort Riley; and served briefly as the Junior Military Aide to President William H. Taft. 'In Memoriam.' *Armor* 65 (March–April 1956), p. 47.
19. 'In Memoriam.'
20. Daniel Van Voorhis, 1st Cavalry Regiment (Mechanized); Memorandum to G-3, 5 May 1931; Files, 1931–41; Willis D. Crittenberger Papers, U.S. Army Army Heritage & Education Center, Carlisle Barracks, Pennsylvania.
21. Memorandum; 'Mechanized Cavalry Division'; Daniel Van Voorhis to Leon B. Kromer, 12 February 1937; Correspondence, 1935–1938; Willis D. Crittenberger Papers; United States Army Army Heritage & Education Center, Carlisle Barracks, PA. Though the .50-caliber machine gun was later recognized primarily as an anti-aircraft weapon, it was originally designed as an anti-tank weapon. Armor plating of tanks, however, soon grew thick enough to easily withstand the .50 round, and other uses were found for the weapon.
22. It is interesting to note that Cold War and early post-Cold War U.S. Army armored divisions contained approximately 500–600 mechanized vehicles.
23. Memorandum; 'Mechanized Cavalry Division'.
24. *Ibid.*
25. *Ibid.*
26. Gillie, pp. 112–13.
27. In 1912, Henry was a member of the U.S. team at the Stockholm Summer Olympics and was awarded the Bronze medal in Equestrian Team Eventing.
28. *Order of Battle of the United States Land Forces in the World War*, Volume 3, Part 2, pp. 651–653.
29. *Ibid*., pp. 811–813.
30. He was on the staff of the Adjutant General's Office, Washington, DC; a student at the Army War College, Washington, DC; a student at School of the Line, Fort Leavenworth; an instructor of Reserve Officers, Camp Devens, Massachusetts; a student at the General Staff School, Fort Leavenworth; the Assistant Commandant of the Cavalry School, Fort Riley; the Chief of Staff of the Philippine Department, Manila; and the commander of the 3rd Cavalry Regiment, Fort Myer, Virginia. Guy V. Henry, Jr.; Career Highlights. Cullum Number 3853. Guy V. Henry, Jr., Papers. Archives of the United States Military Academy, West Point, New York.
31. G. V. Henry, Jr., 'Trend of Organization and Equipment of Cavalry in the Principal World Powers and Its Probable Role in Wars of the Near Future.' *Cavalry Journal* 41 (March–April 1932), p. 9.
32. *Ibid*., p. 8.
33. Letter; Selwyn D. Smith to Guy V. Henry, Jr., 10 December 1932; Correspondence, 1921–1942; Office of the Chief of Cavalry, Record Group 177; National Archives and Records Administration, College Park, Maryland.
34. Letter; Guy V. Henry, Jr., to Abraham G. Lott, 21 March 1933; Correspondence, 1921–1942; Office of the Chief of Cavalry, Record Group 177; National Archives and Records Administration, College Park, Maryland.
35. Letter; Abraham G. Lott to Guy V. Henry, Jr., 24 April 1933; Correspondence, 1921–1942; Office of the Chief of Cavalry, Record Group 177; National Archives and Records Administration, College Park, Maryland.
36. Unpublished Autobiography, p. 68; Guy V. Henry, Jr. Papers; United States Army Army Heritage & Education Center, Carlisle Barracks, PA.
37. *Order of Battle of the United States Land Forces in the World War*, Volume 1, p. 193.
38. *Ibid*., p. 81.

39. He was: on the staff of the Adjutant General's Office, Washington, DC; the G-3 and then G-1, VIII Corps, Ft. Sam Houston, Texas; a member of the G-3 Department, War Department General Staff, Washington, DC; a student at the Army War College, Washington, DC; the commander of the 11th Cavalry Regiment, Presidio of Monterey, California; an instructor at the Army War College; and the Deputy Chief of Staff, First Army, Governor's Island, New York. Leon B. Kromer; Career Highlights. Cullum Number 3889. Leon B. Kromer Papers. Archives of the United States Military Academy, West Point, New York.
40. Leon B. Kromer; 'Lecture on Cavalry'; 17 September 1934. Leon B. Kromer Papers, United States Army Army Heritage & Education Center, Carlisle Barracks, PA.
41. Letter; Leon B. Kromer to John H. Hughes; 19 December 1934; Correspondence, 1921–1942; Office of the Chief of Cavalry, Record Group 177; National Archives and Records Administration, College Park, Maryland.
42. Letter; John H. Hughes to Leon B. Kromer; 11 February 1935; Correspondence, 1921–1942; Office of the Chief of Cavalry, Record Group 177; National Archives and Records Administration, College Park, Maryland.
43. Letter; Leon B. Kromer to John H. Hughes; 27 February 1935; Correspondence, 1921–1942; Office of the Chief of Cavalry, Record Group 177; National Archives and Records Administration, College Park, Maryland.
44. Cameron, *Mobility, Shock, and Firepower: The Emergence of the U.S. Army's Armor Branch, 1917–1945* (2008), p. 69.
45. Memorandum; 'Mechanized Cavalry Division'; Leon B. Kromer to Daniel Van Voorhis, 7 December 1936; Correspondence, 1935–1938; Willis D. Crittenberger Papers; United States Army Army Heritage & Education Center, Carlisle Barracks, PA.
46. Letter; Leon B. Kromer to Willis D. Crittenberger, 16 March 1937; Correspondence, 1935–1938; Willis D. Crittenberger Papers; United States Army Army Heritage & Education Center, Carlisle Barracks, PA.
47. Emphasis added by Kromer. Leon B. Kromer; Lecture on Cavalry; 1 October 1937; Speeches, Articles, Clippings, and Programs; Leon B. Kromer Papers; United States Army Army Heritage & Education Center, Carlisle Barracks, PA.
48. *Ibid.*
49. Grow, pp. 71–74.
50. Memorandum; 'Completion of the Organization of the 7th Cavalry Brigade (Mecz.) by Mechanizing One Horse Cavalry Regiment at Fort Riley, Kansas'; Guy V. Henry, Jr., to Leon B. Kromer, 9 May 1936; Correspondence, 1921–1942; Office of the Chief of Cavalry, Record Group 177; National Archives and Records Administration, College Park, Maryland.
51. Scott became a major general and the commander of the 2nd Armored Division during World War II. Grow, p. 93.

Chapter 5

1. The best interwar memoir from one of the cavalry "pragmatists" is Truscott, *Twilight of the U.S. Cavalry: Life in the Old Army, 1917–1942* (1989).
2. Nenninger, 'Creating Officers: The Leavenworth Experience, 1920–1940', *Military Review* 69 (November 1989), pp. 61–63.
3. Nenninger, 'Brief Account of the Evolution of the Regular Course at the U.S. Army Command and General Staff College', (1988), p. 6.
4. *Ibid.*, p. 7.
5. *Ibid.*, p. 8.
6. *Ibid.*, p. 9.
7. The exact figure is 9.1 percent. This number was derived from a combination of the annual *Army Register* and the annual reports of the CGSS.

8. The Command and General Staff School became the Command and General Staff College in 1947.
9. Davidson, 'Class Standing at CGSC as a Measure of Potential Value to the Service' (1955).
10. The one exception was Hobart R. Gay, a non-West Point graduate, who was commissioned as a cavalry officer during World War I. Gay later transferred to the Quartermaster Corps and graduated from the Army Industrial College which, at the time, was a CGSS alternative for support officers. *Ibid.*
11. Pierce, 'Place of a Mechanized Force in Our Cavalry Organization' (1932), p. 1.
12. *Ibid.*
13. McNeill, 'Critical Analysis of the Pamphlet "Cavalry (Mechanized)", the Command and General Staff College, 1933' (1934), pp. 1–15.
14. Curry, Jr., 'Strength, Composition, Missions, and Sphere of Action of Armored Car Reconnaissance Detachments and Horse Cavalry Reconnaissance Detachments' (1936), p. 7.
15. Bonsteel, 'Employment of Mechanized Cavalry' (1933), pp. 2–3.
16. Pierce, p. 2.
17. *Ibid.*, pp. 17–20.
18. Bals, 'Organization and Employment of a Cavalry Mechanized Force' (1932), pp. 2–3.
19. *Ibid.*, pp. 12–14.
20. *Ibid.*, p. 2.
21. Roffe, 'Study of the Organization of the Cavalry Division' (1931), pp. 10–12.
22. *Ibid.*
23. It is also important to note the size of these formations: horse cavalry division, 9,595 soldiers; infantry division, 22,070 soldiers; and mechanized cavalry brigade, 2,200 soldiers. Dissinger, 'Use of Shock Action by Forces Composed of a Combination of Horse Cavalry and Mechanized Cavalry' (1936), pp. 18–19.
24. *Ibid.*, pp. 21–32.
25. *Ibid.*, pp. 21–24.
26. *Ibid.*, pp. 26–27.
27. *Ibid.*, pp. 28–32.
28. Pierce, pp. 6–17.
29. *Ibid.*, pp. 17–20.
30. Curry, pp. 15–39.
31. Bonsteel, pp. 3–28.
32. Whittaker, 'How Should Armored Cars Be Employed, Particularly with Cavalry, and What Are the General Specifications as to the Types of Cars Required?' (1930), pp. 11–12.
33. Frizzell, 'Equipment for Mechanized Cavalry' (1932), p. 3.
34. Blount, 'Study in Mechanization: The Place in Our Cavalry Organization, Where It Should Be Assigned' (1932), p. 2.
35. *Ibid.*, pp. 6–9.
36. McNeill, pp. 1–3.
37. Dissinger, p. 17.
38. Whittaker, p. 3.
39. *Ibid.*, pp. 4–7.
40. Roffe, pp. 10–12.
41. Pierce, pp. 6–17.
42. *Ibid.*, pp. 17–20.
43. Roffe, pp. 1–2.
44. *Ibid.*, pp. 2–10.
45. Curry, pp. 15–39.
46. Blount, pp. 4–9.
47. *Ibid.*, pp. 6–9.

48. *Ibid.*, pp. 6–9.
49. All of these beliefs, however, were based on the ability of the U.S. Army to procure vehicles, weapons, and other equipment to perform the necessary tasks. Frizzell, pp. 1–2.
50. McNeill, pp. 1–3.
51. Blount, p. 2; and Dissinger, p. 1.
52. Dissinger, p. 3.
53. *Ibid.*, p. 9.
54. Roffe, p. 3.
55. *Ibid.*, pp. 8–9.
56. Bals, pp. 5–12.
57. Frizzell, p. 3.
58. *Ibid.*, pp. 4–13.
59. Whittaker, pp. 13–16.
60. *Ibid.*, pp. 16–19.
61. *Ibid.*, pp. 20–22.
62. Barnes, 'Necessity for Coordination of Reconnaissance Activities of a Cavalry Division–Aviation–Armored Car' (1936), pp. 1–8.
63. *Ibid.*, p. 16.

Chapter 6

1. Martin Blumenson, the foremost scholar of Patton's life and career, directly contrasted Patton's actions in this regard with those of Fuller and Mitchell. Blumenson, ed., *Patton Papers*, Volume I (1972), p. 717.
2. *Ibid.*, p. 88.
3. For a discussion of the development, use, and demise of the U.S. Army's cavalry saber during the twentieth century, see: Turner, *Last Bright Blades: A Study of the Development and the Demise of the Cavalry Saber from 1904–1934* (1982).
4. Blumenson, pp. 331–337.
5. *Ibid.*, p. 435.
6. *Ibid.*, p. 597.
7. *Ibid.*, pp. 619–620.
8. *Ibid.*, p. 645.
9. During most of the wars in American history prior to World War I, volunteer and militia formations had been the dominant manpower source, since the Regular Army was historically so small. Though a draft existed during the Civil War, World War I was the first American conflict in which most American soldiers were drafted. The National Army was a combination of the Regular Army, National Guard, and divisions filled with draftees.
10. During this period, Patton was the commander of the 3rd Squadron, 3rd Cavalry Regiment at Fort Myer; a student in the Advanced Officer's Course at the Cavalry School, Fort Riley; a student (and Honor Graduate) at the Command and General Staff School, Fort Leavenworth, Kansas; the G-1, I Corps Headquarters, Fort Devens, Massachusetts; a staff officer in the Office of the Chief of Cavalry; a student (and Distinguished Graduate) at the Army War College, Washington, DC; the executive officer of the 3rd Cavalry Regiment; and the executive officer of both the Academic Division of the Cavalry School and the 9th Cavalry Regiment at Fort Riley. In July 1938, twenty years after having been promoted to colonel in the Tank Corps, Patton was promoted to colonel in the cavalry and given command of the 3rd Cavalry Regiment at Fort Myer. Blumenson, pp. 968–970.
11. *Ibid.*, p. 642.
12. *Ibid.*, p. 654.
13. *Ibid.*, pp. 660–663.

14. *Ibid.*, p. 680.
15. "Although mortars had been in use for centuries, they were typically extremely large and heavy siege-type weapons that were not easily transportable. Mortars were curved-trajectory weapons that could lob shells into trenches whose occupants would be unaffected by flat trajectory weapons but, compared to standard artillery, mortars had a relatively short range.... The Stokes mortar shell was loaded by dropping a shell down the tube barrel. The shell fired by means of a shotgun-like blank cartridge that exploded when it hit a fixed firing pin attached to the base cap. The exploding cartridge ignited propellant rings attached to the shell." Canfield, *U.S. Infantry Weapons of World War I* (2000), pp. 247–8.
16. Blumenson, p. 703.
17. *Ibid.*, p. 703.
18. *Ibid.*, p. 705.
19. *Ibid.*, pp. 729–731.
20. The Superior Board was established to determine what lessons in tactics, organization, and equipment had been learned during World War I, and how these lessons could be applied to the U.S. Army in anticipation of future conflicts.
21. *Report of the Superior Board on Organization and Tactics*; American Expeditionary Forces-General Headquarters, Chaumont, France; 19 April 1919; Archives of the Command and General Staff College; Fort Leavenworth, Kansas.
22. For the development of anti-tank formations in the U.S. Army, see: Gabel, *Seek, Strike, and Destory: U.S. Army Tank Destroyer Doctrine in World War II* (1985).
23. Blumenson, p. 717.
24. Bradford G. Chynoweth, 'Cavalry Tanks', *Cavalry Journal*, 30 (July 1921), p. 248.
25. *Ibid.*, pp. 250–251.
26. George S. Patton, Jr., 'Comments on "Cavalry Tanks"', *Cavalry Journal* 30 (July 1921), p. 251; and Letter; George S. Patton, Jr., to Bradford G. Chynoweth; 8 March 1921; Memoirs, 1890–1941; Bradford G. Chynoweth Papers; United States Army Army Heritage & Education Center, Carlisle Barracks, PA.
27. Patton, 'Comments on "Cavalry Tanks"', p. 252.
28. G. S. Patton, Jr., 'What the World War Did For Cavalry', *Cavalry Journal* 31 (April 1922), p. 165.
29. *Ibid.*, p. 172.
30. *Ibid.*, p. 165.
31. *Ibid.*, p. 175.
32. *Ibid.*, p. 169.
33. *Ibid.*, p. 171.
34. G. S. Patton, Jr., 'Armored Cars with Cavalry', *Cavalry Journal* 33 (January 1924), pp. 5–6.
35. *Ibid.*, p. 6.
36. *Ibid.*, p. 6.
37. *Ibid.*, p. 8.
38. *Ibid.*, p. 8.
39. 'Cavalry Adopts Armored Cars', *Cavalry Journal* 37 (April 1928), p. 300.
40. C. C. Benson and G. S. Patton, Jr., 'Mechanization and Cavalry', *Cavalry Journal* 39 (April 1930), pp. 235–237.
41. *Ibid.*, pp. 237–238.
42. *Ibid.*, pp. 238–239.
43. *Ibid.*, p. 235.
44. *Ibid.*, p. 240.
45. George S. Patton, Jr.; Memorandum to the Assistant Commandant of the Army War College; 29 February 1932; pp. 1–5; Archives of the Army War College; Carlisle Barracks, Pennsylvania.
46. Patton, 'Probable Characteristics of the Next War and the Organization, Tactics, and Equipment Necessary to Meet Them', pp. 43–45.

47. *Ibid.*, pp. 46–55.
48. G. S. Patton, Jr., 'Mechanized Forces', *Cavalry Journal* 42 (September/October 1933), p. 6.
49. *Ibid.*, p. 6.
50. *Ibid.*, p. 7.
51. Blumenson, p. 953.
52. *Ibid.*, pp. 953–954.
53. Letter; George S. Patton, Jr., to John K. Herr; 10 September 1940. Cullum Number 4112. George S. Patton, Jr., Papers. Archives of the United States Military Academy, West Point, New York.
54. *Ibid.*
55. Blumenson, *Patton Papers*, Volume II (1974), p. 21.
56. *Ibid.*, p. 21.
57. From 1941 to 1945, Patton was promoted from brigadier general to full general and amassed an incredible combat record in North Africa, Sicily, Italy, Northern France, and Germany.
58. Letter; George S. Patton, Jr., to John K. Herr; 7 July 1945. George S. Patton, Jr., Papers. Cullum Number 4112. Archives of the United States Military Academy, West Point, New York.
59. Letter; George S. Patton, Jr., to John K. Herr; 19 August 1945. George S. Patton, Jr., Papers. Cullum Number 4112. Archives of the United States Military Academy, West Point, New York.
60. *Ibid.*

Chapter 7

1. Stubbs and Connor, pp. 58–74.
2. Morton, *Fall of the Philippines* (1953), p. 22.
3. *Ibid.*, p. 138.
4. Jonathan M. Wainwright IV, *General Wainwright's Story: The Account of Four Years of Humiliating Defeat, Surrender, and Captivity* (1949), p. 39.
5. Morton, p. 305.
6. *Ibid.*, p. 406.
7. *Ibid.*, p. 449.
8. Sawicki, pp. 190–91.
9. For more information on the history of mules in the U.S. Army, see: Essin, *Shavetails and Bell Sharps: The History of the U.S. Army Mule* (1997).
10. Stanton, *Order of Battle: U.S. Army, World War II* (1984), p. 320.
11. These were the 2nd, 3rd, 4th, 6th, 15th, 16th, 29th, 101st, 102nd, 104th, 106th, 107th 113th, and 115th Cavalry Regiments. Stubbs and Connor, 113–253.
12. Stubbs, Connor, and McKenney, *Armor-Cavalry*, Part II: *Army National Guard* (1972), pp. 167–71, 187–89.
13. *Ibid.*, pp. 167–71.
14. "The 5332nd Brigade, also known as the MARS Task Force, had three regiments. One contained the survivors of Merrill's Marauders, which had been reorganized, brought up to strength with replacements from the United States, and re-designated the 475th Infantry Regiment. Another was the 124th Cavalry Regiment, a dismounted former National Guard unit from Texas functioning as infantry. The third, considered to be an elite unit, was the U.S.-trained and -equipped 1st Chinese Regiment (Separate)." The MARS Task Force fought in the Central Burma Campaign under Brigadier General John P. Willey. *Central Burma: U.S. Army Campaigns of World War II* (2003), p. 7.
15. Stubbs, Connor, and McKenney, pp. 187–89.
16. U.S. Army, General Board Report, No. 49, "Tactics, Employment, Technique, Organization, and Equipment of Mechanized Cavalry Units" (1945), p. 7.

17. *Ibid.*
18. Stubbs and Connor, pp. 73–74.
19. Stubbs and Connor, p. 74.
20. General Board Report, No. 49, p. 7.
21. *Ibid.*
22. DiMarco, *U.S. Army's Mechanized Cavalry Doctrine in World War II* (1995), pp. 116–117.
23. DiMarco, p. 117.
24. M3/M5 "Stuart" was the primary light tank in the early and middle portions of the war, while the M24 "Chaffee" was the replacement later in the war. See: Zaloga, *M3 & M5 Stuart Light Tank, 1940–45* (1999) and Zaloga, *M24 Chaffee Light Tank, 1943–85* (2003).
25. In the early part of the war, the primary assault gun was the M8, which was based on the M5 "Stuart" light tank. The M8 mounted a short-barreled 75-mm main gun in an open turret, which incorporated parts of the M4 "Sherman" medium tank's gun mount. Later in the war, two variants of the M4 "Sherman" tank were used in this role. The M4A3(105) was a "Sherman" chassis that mounted a 105-mm Howitzer main gun and the M4A3E2 "Jumbo" was "Sherman" chassis with significantly thicker front armor which made it more survivable in combat. See: Zaloga, *Sherman Medium Tank, 1942–45* (1993).
26. DiMarco, p. 118.
27. *Ibid.*, p. 119.
28. The Jeep was a light (¼ ton), four-wheel-drive, general purpose vehicle. See: Zaloga, *Jeeps, 1941–45* (2005).
29. The M8 or M20 "Greyhound" armored cars differed only in that the M8 had a 37-mm main gun, while the M20 had only a .50-caliber machine gun. See: Zaloga, *M8 Greyhound Light Armored Car, 1941–91* (2002).
30. DiMarco, pp. 120–123.
31. *Ibid.*, pp. 121–122.
32. The decision to use a small main gun was the result of vehicle's early war design, when a 37mm main gun was actually large enough to destroy most tanks. See: Zaloga, *M3 & M5 Stuart Light Tank*, 7.
33. DiMarco, pp. 120–123.
34. B. C. Wright, *1st Cavalry Division in World War II* (1947), pp. 3–4.
35. *Ibid.*, pp. 73–100, 125–156.
36. Stanton, p. 73.
37. Harmon, MacKaye, and MacKaye, pp. 280–82.
38. *Ibid.*, pp. 282–84.
39. The dragoons were cavalry riflemen in order that the regiment remained a purely cavalry organization.
40. General Board Report, No. 49, p. 13.
41. U.S. Army, TO&E 17–51, *Armored Cavalry Regiment (Light)* (1948), p. 3.
42. DiMarco, p. 133.
43. U.S. Army, FM 17–22, *Reconnaissance Platoon and Reconnaissance Company* (1950), p. 3.
44. Stubbs and Connor, p. 75.

Conclusion

1. The U.S. Navy, on the other hand, had a distinctly different attitude and spent the interwar period planning for the inevitable (from their point of view) conflict with Japan in the Pacific.

2. These averages are based on statistics provided in: Griffith, *Men Wanted for the U.S. Army: America's Experience with an All-Volunteer Army Between the World Wars* (1982).
3. *Ibid.*, p. 233.
4. *Ibid.*, p. 239.
5. Gabel, *U.S. Army GHQ Maneuvers of 1941*, p. 8.
6. I would include in this group Adna R. Chaffee, Jr., J.F.C. Fuller, Sir Basil H. Liddell Hart, Heinz Guderian, and C. De Gaulle.
7. Ironically, despite the myths to the contrary, this was almost exactly the case for the German Army in World War II. See: DiNardo, *Mechanized Juggernaut or Military Anachronism?: Horses and the German Army of World War II* (1991).
8. J. M. Wainwright IV, 'Mobility', *Cavalry Journal* 44 (September/October 1935), p. 20.

Bibliography

Primary Sources

Ike Skelton Combined Arms Research Library: Fort Leavenworth, Kansas

Bals, Wilson T., "Organization and Employment of a Cavalry Mechanized Force" (1932)

Barnes, George T., "Necessity for Coordination of Reconnaissance Activities of a Cavalry Division—Aviation—Armored Car" (1936)

Blount, Roy E., "Study in Mechanization: The Place in Our Cavalry Organization, Where It Should Be Assigned" (1932)

Birnn, Roland, "Advisability of Making Attack Aviation and Reconnaissance Aviation an Integral Part of the Cavalry Division" (1933)

Bonsteel, Francis T., "Employment of Mechanized Cavalry" (1933)

Byers, Clovis E., "Comparative Study of American, French, German, English, Japanese, Italian, and Russian Doctrine as to the Value of Permanent Corps Organization for Cavalry" (1936)

Curry, James T., Jr., "Strength, Composition, Missions, and Sphere of Action of Armored Car Reconnaissance Detachments and Horse Cavalry Reconnaissance Detachments" (1936)

Davidson, Garrison H., "Class Standing at CGSC as a Measure of Potential Value to the Service" (1955)

Dissinger, Charles E., "Use of Shock Action by Forces Composed of a Combination of Horse Cavalry and Mechanized Cavalry" (1936)

Frizzell, Lawrence C., "Equipment for Mechanized Cavalry" (1932)

McNeill, Norman, "Critical Analysis of the Pamphlet 'Cavalry (Mechanized)', the Command and General Staff School, 1933" (1934)

Nenninger, Timothy K., "Brief Account of the Evolution of the Regular Course at the U.S. Army Command and General Staff College" (1988)

Pierce, John T., "Place of a Mechanized Force in Our Cavalry Organization" (1932)

Phillips, James H., "Motor Vehicle Maintenance of a Cavalry Brigade, Mechanized" (1935)

Roffe, A. W., "Study of the Organization of the Cavalry Division" (1931)

Thomas, Kramer, "Motorization in the Cavalry Division" (1931)

Whittaker, Frank L., "How Should Armored Cars Be Employed, Particularly with Cavalry, and What Are the General Specifications as to the Types of Cars Required?" (1930)

National Archives and Records Administration: College Park, Maryland

Records of the Headquarters, Commanding General, Army Ground Forces, 1916–1943, Records Group 337.

Records of the Office of the Adjutant General, 1916–1943, Records Group 407.
Records of the Office of the Chief of Staff, 1916–1943, Records Group 194.
Records of the Office of the Chief of Cavalry, 1920–1942, Records Group 177.
Records of the United States Army, Continental Commands, 1821–1920, Records Group 393.
Records of the United States Army, Continental Commands, 1920–1942, Records Group 394.
Records of the United States Army, Overseas Operations and Commands, 1898–1942, Records Group 395.
Records of the United States Regular Army, Mobile Units, 1821–1942, Records Group 391.
Records of the War Department, General and Special Staffs, Records Group 165.

United States Military Academy: West Point, New York

Unpublished Manuscript—Wainwright, Jonathan W. V., *"Skinny": The Personal History of General Jonathan M. Wainwright, The Hero of Bataan and Corregidor.*

United States Army Heritage & Education Center: Carlisle Barracks, Pennsylvania

Patton, George S., Jr., "Probable Characteristics of the Next War and the Organization, Tactics, and Equipment Necessary to Meet Them" (1932)
Unpublished Manuscript—Grow, Robert W., *Ten Lean Years: From the Mechanized Force (1930) to the Armored Force (1940).*

Published Materials

Admiralties: Operations of the 1st Cavalry Division, 29 February–18 May 1944 (Washington, D.C.: U.S. Army Center of Military History, 1946)
Armor (Fort Knox, KY: Armor School, 1948–Present)
Army Register (Washington, D.C.: Government Printing Office, 1919–1939)
Bland, L. I., (ed.), *Papers of George Catlett Marshall*, Vols. I–III (Baltimore: Johns Hopkins University Press, 1981–86)
Blumenson, M., (ed.), *Patton Papers*, 2 Vols. (Boston: Houghton Mifflin, 1972–74)
Cavalry Journal (Fort Riley, KS: Cavalry School, 1916–1947)
Cavalry School, United States Army, *Cavalry Combat* (Harrisburg, PA: Telegraph Press, 1937)
Cavalry School, United States Army, *Tactics and Technique of Cavalry, Advanced* (Harrisburg, PA: Military Service Publishing, 1940)
Central Burma: U.S. Army Campaigns of World War II (Washington, D.C.: U.S. Army Center of Military History, 2003)
Chynoweth, B. G., *Bellamy Park* (Hicksville, NY: Exposition Press, 1975)
Clay, S. E., *U.S. Army Order of Battle, 1919–1941*. 4 Volumes (Fort Leavenworth, KS: Combat Studies Institute Press, 2010)
Commandants, Staff, Faculty, and Graduates of the General Service Schools, Fort Leavenworth, Kansas, 1881–1939 (Fort Leavenworth, KS: Command and General Staff School Press, 1939)
Eisenhower, D. D., *At Ease: Stories I Tell My Friends* (Garden City, NY: Doubleday, 1967)
Foulois, B. D., *From the Wright Brothers to the Astronauts: The Memoirs of Major General Benjamin D. Foulois* (New York: McGraw-Hill, 1960)
Gillie, M. H., *Forging the Thunderbolt: A History of the Development of the Armored Force* (Harrisburg, PA: Military Service Publishing, 1947)
Harmon, E. N., M. MacKaye, and W. R. MacKaye. *Combat Commander: Autobiography of a Soldier* (Englewood Cliffs, NJ: Prentice-Hall, 1970)
Herr, J. K., and E. S. Wallace. *Story of the U.S. Cavalry, 1775–1942* (New York: Bonanza Books, 1984)

Howze, H. H., *Cavalryman's Story: Memoirs of a Twentieth-Century Army General* (Washington, D.C.: Smithsonian Institution Press, 1996)
MacArthur, D., *Reminiscences* (New York: McGraw-Hill, 1964)
National Defense Act, Approved June 3, 1913, As Amended by Act Approved June 4, 1920 (Washington, DC: Government Printing Office, 1920)
Order of Battle of the United States Land Forces in the World War. 5 Volumes (Washington, DC: U.S. Army Center of Military History, 1988)
Patton, G. S., Jr., *War As I Knew It* (Boston: Houghton Mifflin, 1947)
Sawicki, J. A., *Cavalry Regiments of the U.S. Army* (Dumfries, VA: Wyvern Publications, 1985)
Stanton, S. L., *Order of Battle: U.S. Army, World War II* (Novato, CA: Presidio Press, 1984)
Stubbs, M. L., and S. R. Connor, *Armor-Cavalry*. Part I: *Regular Army and Army Reserve* (Washington, D.C.: U.S. Army Center of Military History, 1969); and J. E. McKenney, *Armor-Cavalry*. Part II: *Army National Guard* (Washington, DC: U.S. Army Center of Military History, 1972)
Tompkins, F., *Chasing Villa: The Story Behind the Story of Pershing's Expedition Into Mexico* (Harrisburg, PA: Military Service Publishing, 1934)
Truscott, L. K., Jr., *Command Missions: A Personal Story* (New York: E. P. Dutton, 1954); *Twilight of the U.S. Cavalry: Life in the Old Army, 1917–1942* (Lawrence, KS: University Press of Kansas, 1989)
United States Army As A Career (Washington, DC: Government Printing Office, 1929)
U.S. Army, FM 17–22, *Reconnaissance Platoon and Reconnaissance Company* (Washington, DC: Government Printing Office, 1950)
U.S. Army, TO&E 17–51, *Armored Cavalry Regiment (Light)* (Washington, DC: Department of the Army, 1948)
Wainwright, J. M., IV, *General Wainwright's Story: The Account of Four Years of Humiliating Defeat, Surrender, and Captivity* (Garden City, NY: Doubleday, 1949)
Whan, V. E., Jr., ed., *Soldier Speaks: Public Papers and Speeches of General of the Army Douglas MacArthur* (New York: Praeger, 1965)
Willeford, C., *Something About A Soldier* (New York: Random House, 1986)
Wright, B. C., *1st Cavalry Division in World War II* (Tokyo, Japan: Toppan Printing, 1947)
Young, F. E., Jr., *To the Regiment: The History of the 306th Cavalry Regiment and the 306th Armored Cavalry Group* (Washington, D.C.: National Capital Publishing, 1970)

Secondary Sources

Articles and Books

Ambrus, V. G., *Horses in Battle* (Oxford: Oxford University Press, 1975)
Ball, H. P., *Of Responsible Command: A History of the U.S. Army War College* (Carlisle, PA: U.S. Army War College Alumni Association, 1983)
Beaver, D. R., "'Deuce and a Half': Selecting U.S. Army Trucks, 1920–1945" in *Feeding Mars*, (ed.), John A. Lynn, 251–270 (Boulder, CO: Westview, 1993); "Politics and Policy: The War Department Motorization and Standardization Program for Wheeled Transport Vehicles, 1920–1940" in *Military Affairs* 47:3 (October 1983), 101–108.
Bielakowski, A. M., "Role of the Horse in Modern Warfare as Viewed in the Interwar U.S. Army's *Cavalry Journal*" in *Army History: The Professional Bulletin of Army History* No. 50 (Summer–Fall 2000), 20–25; *U.S. Cavalryman, 1891–1920* (Oxford, UK: Osprey Publishing, 2004)
Blackburn, M. K., *United States Army and the Motor Truck: A Case Study in Standardization* (Westport, CT: Greenwood Press, 1996)
Blacker, G. A., *Iron Knights: The United States 66th Armored Regiment, 1918–1945* (Shippensburg, PA: Burd Street Press, 1999)

Blumenson, M., *Patton: The Man Behind the Legend, 1885–1945* (New York: Morrow, 1985); "George S. Patton's Student Days at the Army War College" in *Parameters: Journal of the U.S. Army War College* 5:2 (1976): 25–32

Brereton, J. M., *Horse in War* (New York: Arco Publishing, 1976)

Butterworth, W. E., *Soldiers on Horseback: The Story of the United States Cavalry* (New York: W. W. Norton, 1967)

Cameron, R. S., *Mobility, Shock and Firepower: The Emergence of the U.S. Army's Armor Branch, 1917–1945* (Washington, DC: U.S. Army Center of Military History, 2008)

Canfield, B. N., *U.S. Infantry Weapons of the First World War* (Lincoln, RI: Andrew Mowbray Publishers, 2000); *U.S. Infantry Weapons of World War II* (Lincoln, RI: Andrew Mowbray Publishers, 1994)

Cardozier, V. R., *Mobilization of the United States in World War II: How the Government, Military, and Industry Prepared for War* (Jefferson, NC: McFarland, 1995)

Carroll, J. M., *7th U.S. Cavalry's Own Colonel Tommy Tompkins: A Military Heritage and Tradition* (Bryan, TX: Self-published, 1984)

Chamberlain, P., and C. Ellis. *Pictorical History of Tanks of the World, 1915–45* (Harrisburg, PA: Stackpole Books, 1972)

Chandler, M. C., *Of Garry Owen In Glory: The History of the 7th U.S. Cavalry* (Annadale, VA: Turnpike Press, 1960)

Christie, J. E., *Steel Steeds Christie: A Memoir of J. Walter Christie* (Manhattan, KS: Sunflower University Press, 1985)

Clendenen, C. C., *Blood on the Border: The United States Army and the Mexican Irregulars* (New York: Macmillan, 1969)

Coffman, E. M., *Old Army: A Portrait of the American Army in Peacetime, 1784–1898* (New York: Oxford University Press, 1986); *Regulars: The American Army, 1898–1941* (Cambridge, MA: Belknap Press, 2004); *War to End All Wars: The American Military Experience in World War I* (New York: Oxford University Press, 1968); and P. F. Herrly, "Regular Army Officer Corps Between the World Wars: A Collective Biography" in *Armed Forces and Society* 4:1 (November 1977): 55–73.

Cohen, E. A., "Strategy of Innocence?: The United States, 1920–1945" in *Making of Strategy: Rulers, States, and War*, eds. W. Murray, M. Knox, and A. Bernstein, 428–465 (Cambridge: Cambridge University Press, 1994)

Collier, T. W., "Army and the Great Depression" in *Parameters: Journal of the U.S. Army War College* 18:3 (September 1988): 102–108.

Crosswell, D. K. R., *Chief of Staff: The Military Career of General Walter Bedell Smith* (Westport, CT: Greenwood Press, 1991)

Crow, D., *U.S. Armor-Cavalry, 1917–1967* (Windsor, UK: Profile Publications, 1969)

Dastrup, B. L., *U.S. Army Command and General Staff College: A Centennial History* (Manhattan, KS: Sunflower University Press, 1988)

Daugherty, R. L., *Weathering the Peace: The Ohio National Guard in the Interwar Years, 1919–1940* (Lanham, MD: University Press of America, 1992)

Davies, N., *White Eagle, Red Star: The Polish-Soviet War, 1919–20* (London: Orbis Books, 1983)

D'Este, C., *Patton: A Genius for War* (New York: Harper Collins Publishers, 1995)

DiMarco, L. A., "American Mechanized Cavalry's Critical Contribution to Allied Victory in Europe, 1944–1945" in *Global War Studies: The Journal for the Study of Warfare and Weapons, 1919–1945* 9:2 (2012): 39–66; *War Horse: A History of the Military Horse and Rider* (Yardley, PA: Westholme Publishing, 2008)

DiNardo, R. L., *Mechanized Juggernaut or Military Anachronism?: Horses and the German Army of World War II* (Westport, CT: Greenwood Press, 1991)

Eiler, K. E., *Mobilizing America: Robert P. Patterson and the War Effort, 1940–1945* (Ithaca, NY: Cornell University Press, 1997)

Eisenhower, J. S. D., *Intervention!: The United States and the Mexican Revolution, 1913–1917* (New York: W. W. Norton, 1993)

Ellis, J., *Cavalry: The History of Mounted Warfare* (New York: G.P. Putnam's Sons, 1978)
Eltinge, L., *Notes on Cavalry: Lecture Delivered 14 February 1917* (Fort Leavenworth, KS: Army Service Schools Press, 1917)
Essin, E. M., *Shavetails and Bell Sharps: The History of the U.S. Army Mule* (Lincoln, NE: University of Nebraska Press, 1997)
Farago, L., *Patton: Ordeal and Triumph* (New York: I. Obolensky, 1964)
Forty, G., *U.S. Army Handbook, 1939–1945* (Gloucestershire: Alan Sutton Publishing, 1995)
Gabel, C. R., "1941 Maneuvers: What Did They Really Accomplish?" in *Army History: The Professional Bulletin of Army History* No. 14 (April 1990): 5–7; *Seek, Strike, and Destory: U.S. Army Tank Destroyer Doctrine in World War II* (Fort Leavenworth, KS: Combat Studies Institute Press, 1985); *U.S. Army GHQ Maneuvers of 1941* (Washington, DC: U.S. Army Center of Military History, 1991)
Gott, K. D., *Mobility, Vigilance, and Justice: The U.S. Army Constabulary in Germany, 1946–1953* (Fort Leavenworth, KS: Combat Studies Institute Press, 2006)
Grbasic, Z., and V. Vuksic. *History of Cavalry* (New York: Facts on File, 1989)
Green, C. M., H. C. Thomson, and P. C. Roots, *Ordnance Department: Planning Munitions for War* (Washington, D.C.: U.S. Army Center of Military History, 1955)
Griffith, R. K., Jr., *Men Wanted for the U.S. Army: America's Experience with an All-Volunteer Army Between the World Wars* (Westport, CT: Greenwood Press, 1982)
Hacker, B. C., "Imaginations in Thrall: The Social Psychology of Military Mechanization, 1919–1939" in *Parameters: Journal of the U.S. Army War College* 12:1 (March 1982): 50–61
Hallahan, W. H., *Misfire: The History of How America's Small Arms Have Failed Our Military* (New York: Charles Scribner's Sons, 1994)
Hampton, H. D., *How the U.S. Cavalry Saved Our National Parks* (Bloomington, IN: Indiana University Press, 1971)
Harris, J. P., and F. H., Toase, (eds.), *Armoured Warfare* (London: B.T. Batsford, 1990)
Hewes, J. E., Jr., *From Root to McNamara: Army Organization and Administration, 1900–1963* (Washington, D.C.: U.S. Army Center of Military History, 1975)
Hofmann, G. F., "Demise of the U.S. Tank Corps and Medium Tank Development Program" in *Military Affairs: The Journal of Military History, Including Theory and Technology* 37:1 (February 1973): 20–25; "Tactical and Strategic Use of Attaché Intelligence: The Spanish Civil War and the U.S. Army's Misguided Quest for a Modern Tank Doctrine" in *Journal of Military History* 62:1 (January 1998), 101–134; *Through Mobility We Conquer: The Mechanization of U.S. Cavalry* (Lexington, KY: University of Kentucky Press, 2006); "Yankee Inventor and the Military Establishment: The Christie Tank Controversy" in *Military Affairs: The Journal of Military History, Including Theory and Technology* 39:1 (February 1975): 12–18; and D. A. Starry, (eds.), *Camp Colt to Desert Storm: The History of U.S. Armored Forces* (Lexington, KY: University Press of Kentucky, 1999)
Hooper, F., *Military Horse* (New York: A.S. Barnes, 1976)
House, J. M., *Combined Arms Warfare in the 20th Century* (Lawrence, KS: University Press of Kansas, 2001)
James, D. C., *Years of MacArthur*. Vols. I–II (Boston: Houghton Mifflin, 1970–72)
Jarymowycz, R. J., *Cavalry from Hoof to Track* (Westport, CT: Praeger, 2008)
Johnson, D. E., *Fast Tanks and Heavy Bombers: Innovation in the U.S. Army, 1917–1945.* Ithaca, NY: Cornell University Press, 1998)
Johnson, S., *History of the U.S. Cavalry* (Greenwich, CT: Bison Books, 1985)
Katzenbach, E. L., Jr., "Horse Cavalry in the Twentieth Century" in *The Use of Force: International Politics and Foreign Policy*, eds. R. J. Art and K. N. Waltz, 277–297 (Boston: Little, Brown and Company, 1971); "Tradition and Technological Change" in *American Defense Policy*, (eds.), John F. Reichart and Steven R. Sturm, 638–651 (Baltimore: Johns Hopkins University Press, 1982)
Kaufmann, H. W., and J. E., *Sleeping Giant: American Armed Forces Between the Wars* (Westport, CT: Praeger, 1996)

Killigrew, J. W., *Impact of the Great Depression on the Army* (New York: Garland Publishing, 1979)

Kirkpatrick, C. E., *Unknown Future and a Doubtful Present: Writing the Victory Plan of 1941* (Washington, D.C.: U.S. Army Center of Military History, 1990)

Knapp, G. E., *Buffalo Soldiers at Fort Leavenworth in the 1930's and Early 1940's* (Fort Leavenworth, KS: Combat Studies Institute Press, 1991)

Koistinen, P. A. C., *Planning War, Pursuing Peace: The Political Economy of American Warfare, 1920–1939* (Lawrence, KS: University Press of Kansas, 1998)

Lawford, J., (ed.), *Cavalry* (New York: Crescent Books, 1976)

Liddell Hart, B. H., *Tanks: The History of the Royal Tank Regiment and Its Predecessors—Heavy Machine-Gun Corps, Tank Corps, and Royal Tank Corps, 1914–1945* (New York: Praeger, 1959)

Linn, B. M., *Guardians of Empire: The U.S. Army and the Pacific, 1902–40* (Chapel Hill, NC: University of North Carolina Press, 1997)

Livingston, P., and E. Roberts, *War Horse: Mounting the Cavalry With America's Finest Horses* (Albany, TX: Bright Sky Press, 2003)

Macksey, K., *Tank Pioneers* (New York: Jane's, 1981)

Matloff, M., "American Approach to War, 1919–1945" in, (ed.), M. Howard, *Theory and Practice of War: Essays Presented to Captain B. H. Liddell Hart on his Seventieth Birthday*, 213–243 (New York: Praeger, 1966)

Merrill, J. M., *Spurs to Glory: The Story of the United States Cavalry* (Chicago: Rand McNally, 1964)

Miller, R. G., *Preliminary to War: The 1st Aero Squadron and the Mexican Punitive Expedition of 1916* (Washington, D.C.: Air Force History and Museums Program, 2003)

Millett, A. R., and W. Murray, (eds.), *Military Effectiveness*. Vol. II, *Interwar Period* (Boston: Allen & Unwin, 1988); *Military Innovation in the Interwar Period (New York*: Cambridge University Press, 1996)

Morison, E. E., *Men, Machines, and Modern Times* (Cambridge, MA: Massachusetts Institute of Technology Press, 1966)

Morton, L., *Fall of the Philippines* (Washington, D.C.: U.S. Army Center of Military History, 1953)

Moy, T., *War Machines: Transforming Technologies in the U.S. Military, 1920–1940* (College Station, TX: Texas A&M University Press, 2001)

Nenninger, T. K., "Creating Officers: The Leavenworth Experience, 1920–1940" in *Military Review* 69 (November 1989): 58–68; "Development of Armor, 1917–1940: The World War I Experience" in *Armor* 78 (Jan–Feb 1969): 46–51; "Development of Armor, 1917–1940: The Tank Corps Reorganized" in *Armor* 78 (Mar–Apr 1969): 34–38; "Development of Armor, 1917–1940: The Experimental Mechanized Forces" in *Armor* 78 (May–June 1969): 33–39; "Development of Armor, 1917–1940: A Revised Mechanization Policy" in *Armor* 78 (Sep–Oct 1969): 45–49; "Leavenworth and Its Critics: The U.S. Army Command and General Staff School, 1920–1940" in *Journal of Military History* 58:2 (April 1994): 199–231; *Leavenworth Schools and the Old Army: Education, Professionalism, and the Officer Corps of the United States Army, 1881–1918* (Westport, CT: Greenwood Press, 1978)

Nye, R. H., *Patton Mind: The Professional Development of An Extraordinary Leader* (Garden City Park, NY: Avery Publishing, 1993); "Whence Patton's Military Genius?" in *Parameters: Journal of the U.S. Army War College* 11:4 (Winter 1991–92): 60–73

Odom, W. O., *After the Trenches: The Transformation of U.S. Army Doctrine, 1918–1939* (College Station, TX: Texas A&M University Press, 1999)

Ogorkiewicz, R. M., *Armoured Forces: A History of Armoured Forces and their Vehicles* (London: Arms and Armour Press, 1970)

Piekalkiewicz, J., *Cavalry in World War II* (New York: Stein and Day, 1976)

Pogue, F. C., *George C. Marshall: Education of a General, 1880–1939* (New York: Viking Press, 1963); *George C. Marshall: Ordeal and Hope, 1939–1942* (New York: Viking Press,

1966); *George C. Marshall: Organizer of Victory, 1943–1945* (New York: Viking Press, 1973)

Raborg, P. C., *Mechanized Might: The Story of Mechanized Warfare* (New York: McGraw-Hill, 1942)

Ramsey, E. P., and S. J. Rivele. *Lieutenant Ramsey's War: From Horse Soldier to Guerilla Commander* (Washington, D.C.: Brassey's, 1996)

Reedstrom, E. L., "U.S. Cavalry Tactical Manuals" in *Proceedings of the Colloquium on Military History*, (ed.), C. J. Balesi, 74–84 (Chicago: United States Commission on Military History, 1979)

Reinhardt, G. C., and W. R. Kintner. *Haphazard Years: How America Has Gone to War* (Garden City, NY: Doubleday, 1960)

Schifferle, P. J., *America's School for War: Fort Leavenworth, Officer Education, and Victory in World War II* (Lawrence, KS: University Press of Kansas, 2010)

Schultz, D. P., *Hero of Bataan: The Story of General Jonathan M. Wainwright* (New York: St. Martin's Press, 1981)

Semmes, H. H., *Portrait of Patton* (New York: Appleton-Century-Crofts, 1955)

Simmons, S., (ed.), *Military Horse* (London: Marshall Cavendish Publications, 1976)

Steffen, R., *Horse Soldier, 1776–1943—The United States Cavalryman: His Uniforms, Arms, Accoutrements, and Equipments*. Vol. IV, *World War I, the Peacetime Army, World War II, 1917–1943* (Norman, OK: University of Oklahoma Press, 1979)

Stone, N., *Eastern Front, 1914–1917* (London: Hodder and Stoughton, 1975)

Stout, J. A., Jr., *Border Conflict: Villistas, Carrancistas, and the Punitive Expedition, 1915–1920* (Forth Worth, TX: Texas Christian University Press, 1999)

Sutton, J., and J. Walker, *From Horse to Helicopter* (London: Leo Cooper, 1990)

Turner, J. W., *Last Bright Blades: A Study of the Development and the Demise of the Cavalry Saber from 1904–1934* (Atascadero, CA: Wagapaw Press, 1982)

U.S. Cavalry Association. *We Remember: U.S. Cavalry Association* (Paducah, KY: Turner Publishing, 1996)

Weigley, R. F., *History of the United States Army* (Bloomington, IN: Indiana University Press, 1984); "Interwar Army, 1919–1941" in *Against All Enemies: Interpretations of American Military History from Colonial Times to the Present*, eds. K. J. Hagan and W. R. Roberts, 257–278 (New York: Greenwood Press, 1986); *Towards an American Army: Military Thought From Washington to Marshall* (New York: Columbia University Press, 1962)

Whitman, J. W., "Last U.S. Horse Cavalry Charge" in *Military History* (June 1995): 38–45

Wilson, D. E., *Treat 'em Rough!: The Birth of American Armor, 1917–1929* (Novato, CA: Presidio Press, 1989)

Wilson, J. R. M., "Quaker and the Sword: Herbert Hoover's Relations With the Military" in *Military Affairs* 38:2 (April 1974): 41–47

Winton, H. R., and D. R. Mets. *Challenge to Change: Military Institutions and New Realities, 1918–1941* (Lincoln, NE: University of Nebraska Press, 2000)

Woolley, W. J., "Patton and the Concept of Mechanized Warfare" in *Parameters: Journal of the U.S. Army War College* 15:3 (Autumn 1985): 71–80

Wormser, R., *Yellowlegs: The Story of the United States Cavalry* (Garden City, NY: Doubleday, 1966)

Wrangel, A., *End of Chivalry: The Last Great Cavalry Battles, 1914–1918* (New York: Hippocrene Books, 1982)

Zaloga, S. J., *Jeeps, 1941–45* (Oxford, UK: Osprey Publishing, 2005); *M24 Chaffee Light Tank, 1943–85* (Oxford, UK: Osprey Publishing, 2003); *M3 & M5 Stuart Light Tank, 1940–45* (Oxford, UK: Osprey Publishing, 1999); *M8 Greyhound Light Armored Car, 1941–91* (Oxford, UK: Osprey Publishing, 2002); *Sherman Medium Tank, 1942–45* (Oxford, UK: Osprey Publishing, 1993); and Victor Madej. *Polish Campaign, 1939* (New York: Hippocrene Books, 1985)

Dissertations and Theses

Broom, J. T., *Commander's Vision In Blue and Grey: The Roles of Adna R. Chaffee, Jr., James H. Wilson, and the American Civil War in the Development of American Armor Doctrine* (Ph.D. diss., The Union Institute, 1993)

Cary, N. M., Jr., *Use of the Motor Vehicle in the United States Army, 1899–1939* (Ph.D. diss., University of Georgia, 1980)

Cockrell, P. C., *Brown Shoes and Mortar Boards: U.S. Army Officer Professional Education at the Command and General Staff School, Fort Leavenworth, Kansas, 1919–1940* (Ph.D. diss., University of South Carolina, 1991)

Daley, J. L. S., *From Theory to Practice: Tanks, Doctrine, and the U.S. Army, 1916–1940* (Ph.D. diss., Kent State University, 1993)

DiMarco, L. A., *U.S. Army's Mechanized Cavalry Doctrine in World War II* (M.M.A.S. Thesis, U.S. Army Command and General Staff College, 1995)

Miller, R. A., *United States Army During the 1930's* (Ph.D. diss., Princeton University, 1973)

Nowowiejski, D. A., *Adapation to Change: U.S. Army Cavalry Doctrine and Mechanization, 1938–1945* (M.M.A.S. Thesis, School of Advanced Military Studies, U.S. Army Command and General Staff College, 1995)

Rittgers, S. J., *From Galloping Hooves to Rumbling Engines: Organizational Responses to Technology in the U.S. Horse Cavalry* (Ph.D. diss., George Washington University, 2003)

Turner, F. C., *Genesis of the Soviet "Deep Operation": The Stalin-Era Doctrine for Large-Scale Offensive Maneuver Warfare* (Ph.D. diss., Duke University, 1988)

Biography

Alexander M. Bielakowski is a former U.S. Army Reserve officer who has published on such diverse topics as Polish Americans in the Civil War, African Americans in World War II, Dwight D. Eisenhower as the first commander of NATO, and Vietnam War movies. He has authored or co-authored three monographs as well as edited a two-volume reference work. He spent more than decade educating military officers at the U.S. Army Command and General Staff College, Fort Leavenworth, Kansas. Currently, he is Editor-in-Chief of the peer-reviewed journal *U.S. Military History Review* and a professor at the University of Houston-Downtown.